# Afghan Lover's
# Collection

LEISURE ARTS, INC.
Maumelle, Arkansas

EDITORIAL STAFF
Editor-in-Chief: Susan White Sullivan
Director of Designer Relations: Cheryl Johnson
Special Projects Director: Susan Frantz Wiles
Senior Prepress Director: Mark Hawkins
Art Publications Director: Rhonda Shelby
Technical Editor: Linda A. Daley
Technical Writers: Sarah J. Green, Cathy Hardy,
    and Lois J. Long
Editorial Writer: Susan McManus Johnson
Art Category Manager: Lora Puls
Graphic Artists: Jacob Casleton and
    Becca Snider
Imaging Technician: Stephanie Johnson
Prepress Technician: Janie Marie Wright
Photography Manager: Katherine Laughlin
Contributing Photographer: Ken West
Contributing Photostylist: Sondra Daniel
Publishing Systems Administrator: Becky Riddle
Mac Information Technology Specialist:
    Robert Young

BUSINESS STAFF
President and Chief Executive Officer:
    Rick Barton
Vice President and Chief Operations Officer:
    Tom Siebenmorgen
Vice President of Sales: Mike Behar
Director of Finance and Administration:
    Laticia Mull Dittrich
National Sales Director: Martha Adams
Creative Services: Chaska Lucas
Information Technology Director: Hermine Linz
Controller: Francis Caple
Vice President, Operations: Jim Dittrich
Retail Customer Service Manager: Stan Raynor
Print Production Manager: Fred F. Pruss

Library of Congress Control Number:
    2011921954
ISBN-13: 978-1-60900-128-5

# TABLE OF CONTENTS

There's so much to love about afghans! These patterns to crochet were created by some of Leisure Arts' most popular designers, including Anne Halliday, Melissa Leapman, and Barbara Shaffer. Whether you adore lacy elegance or bold bobbles, unique motifs or original ripples, each exciting design is one-of-a-kind. Enhance your home with the color and warmth of these soft throws. Or create them as wedding, birthday, or friendship gifts. It's fun to indulge your love of crocheted afghans—especially with such tempting textures for inspiration!

# SUNNY TWEED

**MATERIALS**
Medium Weight Yarn
[7 ounces, 364 yards (198 grams, 333 meters) per skein]:
  Dk Blue **and** Blue - 4 skeins **each** color
  White **and** Yellow - 3 skeins **each** color
Crochet hook, size K (6.5 mm) **or** size needed for gauge
Safety pins
Yarn needle

■■□□ EASY +

**Finished Size:** 48" x 67"
(122 cm x 170 cm)

Afghan is worked holding two strands of yarn together.

**GAUGE SWATCH:** One Square = 4³/₄" (12 cm)

## SQUARE (Make 117)
Holding one strand of White and one strand of Yellow together, ch 6; join with slip st to form a ring.

**Rnd 1** (Right side)**:** Ch 3 **(counts as first dc)**, 15 dc in ring; join with slip st to first dc, slip loop from hook onto safety pin to keep piece from unraveling while working next rnd: 16 dc.

**Note:** Loop a short piece of yarn around any stitch to mark Rnd 1 as **right** side.

Keep dropped yarn and safety pin to **wrong** side, now and throughout.

**Rnd 2:** With **right** side facing and holding one strand of Blue and one strand of Dk Blue together, join yarn with sc in joining slip st **(see Joining With Sc, page 122)**; ch 1, skip first dc, (sc in next dc, ch 1) around; join with slip st to first sc, slip loop from hook onto safety pin to keep piece from unraveling while working next rnd: 16 sc and 16 ch-1 sps.

**Rnd 3:** With **wrong** side facing, remove safety pin from Rnd 1 and place loop onto hook; ch 3, sc in ch-1 sp **behind** ch-3, ch 1, (sc in next ch-1 sp, ch 1) around; join with slip st to first sc, finish off.

**Rnd 4:** With **right** side facing and working **behind** Rnd 3, remove safety pin from Rnd 2 and place loop onto hook; ch 3, sc in sc in **front** of ch-3, ch 1, (dc, ch 3, dc) in next sc, ch 1, sc in next sc, ch 1, slip st in next sc, ch 1, ★ sc in next sc, ch 1, (dc, ch 3, dc) in next sc, ch 1, sc in next sc, ch 1, slip st in next sc, ch 1; repeat from ★ 2 times **more**; join with slip st to first sc, finish off: 20 sps.

*Instructions continued on page 11.*

# ONE-OF-A-KIND

**MATERIALS**
Bulky Weight Yarn **[5]**
[6 ounces, 185 yards (170 grams, 169 meters) per skein]:
  Ecru - 12 skeins
  Blue - 5 skeins
Crochet hook, size J (6 mm) **or** size needed for gauge
Safety pin
Yarn needle

■■■□ **INTERMEDIATE**

**Finished Size:** 56" x 74"
(142 cm x 188 cm)

**GAUGE:** Each Square = 6" (15.25 cm)

**Gauge Swatch:** 3" (7.5 cm) square
Work same as Square through Rnd 2.

## STITCH GUIDE

**TREBLE CROCHET** *(abbreviated tr)*
YO twice, insert hook in st or sp indicated, YO and pull up a loop (4 loops on hook), (YO and draw through 2 loops on hook) 3 times.

## SQUARE (Make 88)

With Ecru, ch 5; join with slip st to form a ring.

**Rnd 1** (Right side)**:** Ch 3 **(counts as first dc, now and throughout)**, 2 dc in ring, (ch 3, 3 dc in ring) 3 times, ch 1, hdc in first dc to form last ch-3 sp: 12 dc.

**Note:** Loop a short piece of yarn around any stitch to mark Rnd 1 as **right** side.

**Rnd 2:** Ch 5 **(counts as first tr plus ch 1, now and throughout)**, 2 dc in last ch-3 sp made, dc in next 3 dc, ★ (2 dc, ch 1, tr, ch 1, 2 dc) in next ch-3 sp, dc in next 3 dc; repeat from ★ around, 2 dc in same sp as first tr, ch 1; join with slip st to first tr; place loop from hook onto safety pin to keep piece from unraveling as you work the next rnd: 28 dc and 4 tr.

**Rnd 3:** With **wrong** side facing and keeping safety pin and working yarn on **wrong** side of work, join Blue with sc in ch before any corner tr **(see Joining With Sc, page 122)**; ch 3, skip corner tr, sc in next ch, ch 1, skip next dc, (sc in next dc, ch 1, skip next dc) 3 times, ★ sc in next ch, ch 3, skip next corner tr, sc in next ch, ch 1, skip next dc, (sc in next dc, ch 1, skip next dc) 3 times; repeat from ★ 2 times **more**; join with slip st to first sc, finish off: 20 sc and 20 sps.

*Instructions continued on page 8.*

**Rnd 4:** With **right** side facing and working **behind** corner ch-3, remove safety pin and place Ecru loop onto hook; ch 5, dc in same st as joining on Rnd 2 *(Fig. 7, page 124)*, ch 1, skip next sc on Rnd 3, ★ † working in **front** of next ch-1, dc in skipped dc one rnd **below**, (sc in next sc on Rnd 3, working in **front** of next ch-1, dc in skipped dc one rnd **below**) 3 times, ch 1, skip next sc on Rnd 3 †, working **behind** next corner ch-3, (dc, ch 1, tr, ch 1, dc) in corner tr one rnd **below**, ch 1, skip next sc on Rnd 3; repeat from ★ 2 times **more**, then repeat from † to † once, working **behind** corner ch-3, dc in same corner tr as first tr, ch 1; join with slip st to first tr, place loop from hook onto safety pin: 40 sts and 16 ch-1 sps.

**Rnd 5:** With **wrong** side facing and keeping safety pin and working yarn on **right** side of work, join Blue with sc in ch before any corner tr; ★ † ch 3, skip corner tr, sc in next ch, ch 1, skip next dc, working **behind** next ch-1, dc in skipped sc one rnd **below**, ch 1, skip next dc on Rnd 4, (sc in next sc, ch 1, skip next dc) 3 times, working **behind** next ch-1, dc in skipped sc one rnd **below**, ch 1, skip next dc on Rnd 4 †, sc in next ch; repeat from ★ 2 times **more**, then repeat from † to † once; join with slip st to first sc, finish off: 28 sts and 28 sps.

**Rnd 6:** With **right** side facing and working in **front** of corner ch-3, remove safety pin and place Ecru loop onto hook; ch 3, ★ † sc in next sc on Rnd 5, working in **front** of next ch-1, dc in skipped dc one rnd **below**, sc in next dc on Rnd 5, (working **behind** next ch-1, dc in skipped dc one rnd **below**, sc in next st on Rnd 5) 4 times, working in **front** of next ch-1, dc in skipped dc one rnd **below**, sc in next sc on Rnd 5 †, working in **front** of next corner ch-3, (dc, ch 3, dc) in corner tr one rnd **below**; repeat from ★ 2 times **more**, then repeat from † to † once, working in **front** of corner ch-3, dc in same st as first dc, ch 3; join with slip st to first dc, finish off: 60 sts and 4 ch-3 sps.

## ASSEMBLY

With Ecru and working through **both** loops on **both** pieces, whipstitch Squares together forming 8 vertical strips of 11 Squares each *(Fig. 9a, page 125)*, beginning in center ch of first corner ch-3 and ending in center ch of next corner ch-3; then whipstitch strips together in same manner.

## EDGING

When working into chains, work into top 2 loops of each chain *(Fig. A)*.

**Fig. A**

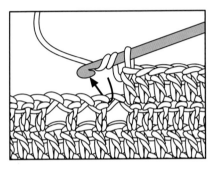

**Rnd 1:** With **right** side facing, join Ecru with dc in any corner ch-3 sp *(see Joining With Dc, page 122)*; (dc, ch 1, tr, ch 1, 2 dc) in same sp, ★ † dc in next 15 sts, (dc in next ch, dc in joining and in next ch, dc in next 15 sts) across to next corner ch-3 sp †, (2 dc, ch 1, tr, ch 1, 2 dc) in corner ch-3 sp; repeat from ★ 2 times **more**, then repeat from † to † once; join with slip st to first dc, finish off: 692 sts and 8 ch-1 sps.

**Rnd 2:** With **wrong** side facing, join Blue with sc in ch before any corner tr; ★ † ch 3, skip corner tr, sc in next ch, ch 1, skip next dc, (sc in next dc, ch 1, skip next dc) across to next corner †, sc in next ch; repeat from ★ 2 times **more**, then repeat from † to † once; join with slip st to first sc, finish off: 350 sc and 350 sps.

**Rnd 3:** With **right** side facing, join Ecru with sc in same sc as joining slip st; ★ † (working **behind** next ch-1, dc in skipped dc one rnd **below**, sc in next sc on Rnd 2) across to next corner ch-3, working **behind** corner ch-3, (dc, ch 1, tr, ch 1, dc) in corner tr one rnd **below** †, sc in next sc on Rnd 2; repeat from ★ 2 times **more**, then repeat from † to † once; join with slip st to first sc, finish off: 708 sts and 8 sps.

**Rnd 4:** With **wrong** side facing, join Blue with sc in ch before any corner tr; ★ † ch 3, skip corner tr, sc in next ch, ch 1, skip next dc, (sc in next sc, ch 1, skip next dc) across to next corner †, sc in next ch; repeat from ★ 2 times **more**, then repeat from † to † once; join with slip st to first sc, finish off: 358 sc and 358 sps.

**Rnd 5:** With **right** side facing, join Ecru with sc in sc before any corner ch-3; ★ † working in **front** of corner ch-3, (dc, ch 1, tr, ch 1, dc) in corner tr one rnd **below**, [(sc in next sc on Rnd 4, working in **front** of next ch-1, dc in skipped dc one rnd **below**) 4 times, ch 1, skip next sc on Rnd 4, working **behind** next ch-1, dc in skipped dc one rnd **below**, (sc in next sc on Rnd 4, working **behind** next ch-1, dc in skipped dc one rnd **below**) 3 times, ch 1, skip next sc on Rnd 4, working in **front** of next ch-1, dc in skipped dc one rnd **below**] across to within 3 ch-1 sps of next corner ch-3, (sc in next sc on Rnd 4, working in **front** of next ch-1, dc in skipped dc one rnd **below**) 3 times †, sc in next sc on Rnd 4; repeat from ★ 2 times **more**, then repeat from † to † once; join with slip st to first sc, finish off: 724 sts and 8 sps.

**Rnd 6:** With **wrong** side facing, join Blue with sc in ch after any corner tr; ★ † ch 1, skip next dc, (sc in next sc, ch 1, skip next dc) 4 times, [working **behind** next ch-1, dc in skipped sc one rnd **below**, ch 1, skip next dc on Rnd 5, (sc in next sc, ch 1, skip next dc) 3 times, working **behind** next ch-1, dc in skipped sc one rnd **below**, ch 1, skip next dc on Rnd 5, (sc in next sc, ch 1, skip next dc) 4 times] across to next corner, sc in next ch, ch 3, skip corner tr †, sc in next ch; repeat from ★ 2 times **more**, then repeat from † to † once; join with slip st to first sc, finish off: 366 sts and 366 sps.

**Rnd 7:** With **right** side facing, join Ecru with sc in sc before any corner ch-3; ★ † working **behind** corner ch-3, (dc, ch 1, tr, ch 1, dc) in corner tr one rnd **below**, (sc in next sc on Rnd 6, working **behind** next ch-1, dc in skipped dc one rnd **below**) 5 times, [ch 1, skip next dc on Rnd 6, working in **front** of next ch-1, dc in skipped dc one rnd **below**, (sc in next sc on Rnd 6, working in **front** of next ch-1, dc in skipped dc one rnd **below**) 3 times, ch 1, skip next dc on Rnd 6, working **behind** next ch-1, dc in skipped dc one rnd **below**, (sc in next sc on Rnd 6, working **behind** next ch-1, dc in skipped dc one rnd **below**) 4 times] across to within one sc of next corner ch-3 †, sc in next sc; repeat from ★ 2 times **more**, then repeat from † to † once; join with slip st to first sc, finish off: 740 sts and 8 sps.

**Rnd 8:** With **wrong** side facing, join Blue with sc in ch before any corner tr; ★ † ch 3, skip corner tr, sc in next ch, ch 1, skip next dc, (sc in next sc, ch 1, skip next dc) 5 times, working **behind** next ch-1, dc in skipped dc one rnd **below**, ch 1, skip next dc on Rnd 7, (sc in next sc, ch 1, skip next dc) 3 times, working **behind** next ch-1, dc in skipped dc one rnd **below**, ch 1, [skip next dc on Rnd 7, (sc in next sc, ch 1, skip next dc) 4 times, working **behind** next ch-1, dc in skipped dc one rnd **below**, ch 1, skip next dc on Rnd 7, (sc in next sc, ch 1, skip next dc) 3 times, working **behind** next ch-1, dc in skipped dc one rnd **below**, ch 1] across to within 11 sts of first ch-1 of next corner, skip next dc, (sc in next sc, ch 1, skip next dc) 5 times †, sc in next ch; repeat from ★ 2 times **more**, then repeat from † to † once; join with slip st to first sc, finish off: 374 sts and 374 sps.

*Instructions continued on page 10.*

continued from ONE-OF-A-KIND page 6

**Rnd 9:** With **right** side facing, join Ecru with sc in sc before any corner ch-3 sp; ★ † working in **front** of corner ch-3, (dc, ch 1, tr, ch 1, dc) in corner tr one rnd **below**, (sc in next sc on Rnd 8, working in **front** of next ch-1, dc in skipped dc one rnd **below**) 6 times, (sc in next st on Rnd 8, working **behind** next ch-1, dc in skipped dc one rnd **below**) 4 times, [(sc in next st on Rnd 8, working in **front** of next ch-1, dc in skipped dc one rnd **below**) 5 times, (sc in next st on Rnd 8, working **behind** next ch-1, dc in skipped dc one rnd **below**) 4 times] across to within 6 ch-1 sps of next corner ch-3, (sc in next st on Rnd 8, working in **front** of next ch-1, dc in skipped dc one rnd **below**) 6 times †, sc in next sc on Rnd 8; repeat from ★ 2 times **more**, then repeat from † to † once; join with slip st to first sc, finish off: 756 sts and 8 sps.

**Rnd 10:** With **wrong** side facing, join Blue with sc in ch before any corner tr; ★ † ch 3, skip corner tr, sc in next ch, ch 1, skip next dc, (sc in next sc, ch 1, skip next dc) across to next corner †, sc in next ch; repeat from ★ 2 times **more**, then repeat from † to † once; join with slip st to first sc, finish off: 382 sc and 382 sps.

**Rnd 11:** With **right** side facing, join Ecru with sc in same sc as joining slip st; ★ † (working **behind** next ch-1, dc in skipped dc one rnd **below**, sc in next sc on Rnd 10) across to next corner ch-3, working **behind** corner ch-3, (dc, ch 1, tr, ch 1, dc) in corner tr one rnd **below** †, sc in next sc on Rnd 10; repeat from ★ 2 times **more**, then repeat from † to † once; join with slip st to first sc, finish off: 772 sts and 8 sps.

**Rnd 12:** Ch 1, turn; sc in same st as joining, ch 1, skip next dc, sc in next ch, ch 1, sc in next tr, ch 1, sc in next ch, ch 1, ★ skip next dc, (sc in next sc, ch 1, skip next dc) across to next corner ch-1, sc in next ch, ch 1, sc in next tr, ch 1, sc in next ch, ch 1; repeat from ★ 2 times **more**, skip next dc, (sc in next sc, ch 1, skip next dc) across; join with slip st to first sc.

**Rnd 13:** Ch 1, turn; (slip st in next ch-1 sp, ch 2) around; join with slip st to first slip st, finish off.

*Design by Anne Halliday.*

## ASSEMBLY

With one strand of Dk Blue and working through **both** loops on **both** pieces, whipstitch Squares together *(Fig. 9a, page 125)*, forming 9 vertical strips of 13 Squares each, beginning in center ch of first corner ch-3 and ending in center ch of next corner ch-3; whipstitch strips together in same manner.

## EDGING

**Rnd 1:** With **right** side facing and holding one strand of Blue and one strand of Dk Blue together, join yarn with sc in any corner ch-3 sp; ch 2, sc in same sp, ch 1, ★ (sc in next sp, ch 1) across to next corner ch-3 sp, (sc, ch 2, sc) in corner ch-3 sp, ch 1; repeat from ★ 2 times **more**, (sc in next sp, ch 1) across; join with slip st to first sc: 264 sc and 264 sps.

**Rnd 2:** Ch 1, turn; ★ (sc in next ch-1 sp, ch 1) across to next corner ch-2 sp, (sc, ch 2, sc) in corner ch-2 sp, ch 1; repeat from ★ around; join with slip st to first sc, slip loop from hook onto safety pin to keep piece from unraveling while working next rnd: 268 sc and 268 sps.

**Rnd 3:** With **right** side facing and holding one strand of White and one strand of Yellow together, join yarn with sc in any corner ch-2 sp; ch 2, sc in same sp, ch 1, ★ (sc in next ch-1 sp, ch 1) across to next corner ch-2 sp, (sc, ch 2, sc) in corner ch-2 sp, ch 1; repeat from ★ 2 times **more**, (sc in next ch-1 sp, ch 1) across; join with slip st to first sc, slip loop from hook onto safety pin to keep piece from unraveling while working next rnd: 272 sc and 272 sps.

**Rnd 4:** With **wrong** side facing, remove safety pin from Rnd 2 and place loop onto hook; ch 2, sc in ch-1 sp **behind** ch-2, ch 1, ★ (sc in next ch-1 sp, ch 1) across to next corner ch-2 sp, (sc, ch 2, sc) in corner ch-2 sp, ch 1; repeat from ★ 3 times **more**, sc in last ch-1 sp, ch 1; join with slip st to first sc, slip loop from hook onto safety pin to keep piece from unraveling while working next rnd: 276 sc and 276 sps.

**Rnd 5:** With **right** side facing and working **behind** Rnd 4, remove safety pin from Rnd 3 and place loop onto hook; ch 2, sc in ch-1 sp in **front** of ch-2, ch 1, (sc, ch 2, sc) in next corner ch-2 sp, ch 1, ★ (sc in next ch-1 sp, ch 1) across to next corner ch-2 sp, (sc, ch 2, sc) in corner ch-2 sp, ch 1; repeat from ★ 2 times **more**, (sc in next ch-1 sp, ch 1) across; join with slip st to first sc, finish off: 280 sc and 280 sps.

**Rnd 6:** With **wrong** side facing, remove safety pin from Rnd 4 and place loop onto hook; ch 2, sc in ch-1 sp **behind** ch-2, ch 1, ★ (sc in next ch-1 sp, ch 1) across to next corner ch-2 sp, (sc, ch 2, sc) in corner ch-2 sp, ch 1; repeat from ★ 3 times **more**, (sc in next ch-1 sp, ch 1) twice; join with slip st to first sc: 284 sc and 284 sps.

**Rnd 7:** Ch 1, turn; ★ (slip st in next ch-1 sp, ch 1) across to next corner ch-2 sp, (slip st, ch 2, slip st) in corner ch-2 sp, ch 1; repeat from ★ 3 times **more**, (slip st in next ch-1 sp, ch 1) across; join with slip st to first slip st, finish off.

*Design by Anne Halliday.*

# GLIMPSE OF GRANNY

**MATERIALS**

Medium Weight Yarn [4]
[5 ounces, 256 yards (140 grams, 234 meters) per skein]:
  White - 7 skeins
  Green - 2 skeins
  Purple - 2 skeins
  Teal - 1 skein
Crochet hook, size I (5.5 mm) **or** size needed for gauge
Yarn needle

▬▬▬▬▭ **INTERMEDIATE**

**Finished Size:** 47" x 68"
(119.5 cm x 172.5 cm)

**GAUGE:** Each Square = 5¼" (13.25 cm)

**Gauge Swatch:** 3" (7.5 cm) square
Work same as Square A through Rnd 2.

## SQUARE A (Make 39)

**Rnd 1** (Right side): With Teal, ch 4, 2 dc in fourth ch from hook, ch 3, (3 dc in same ch, ch 3) 3 times; join with slip st to top of beginning ch-4, finish off: 12 sts and 4 ch-3 sps.

**Note:** Loop a short piece of yarn around any stitch to mark Rnd 1 as **right** side.

**Rnd 2:** With **right** side facing, join Purple with dc in any ch-3 sp **(see Joining With Dc, page 122)**; (2 dc, ch 3, 3 dc) in same sp, ch 1, ★ (3 dc, ch 3, 3 dc) in next ch-3 sp, ch 1; repeat from ★ 2 times **more**; join with slip st to first dc, finish off: 24 dc and 8 sps.

**Rnd 3:** With **right** side facing, join Green with dc in any corner ch-3 sp; (2 dc, ch 3, 3 dc) in same sp, ch 1, 3 dc in next ch-1 sp, ch 1, ★ (3 dc, ch 3, 3 dc) in next corner ch-3 sp, ch 1, 3 dc in next ch-1 sp, ch 1; repeat from ★ 2 times **more**; join with slip st to first dc, finish off: 36 dc and 12 sps.

**Rnd 4:** With **right** side facing, join White with dc in any corner ch-3 sp; (2 dc, ch 3, 3 dc) in same sp, ch 1, (3 dc in next ch-1 sp, ch 1) twice, ★ (3 dc, ch 3, 3 dc) in next corner ch-3 sp, ch 1, (3 dc in next ch-1 sp, ch 1) twice; repeat from ★ 2 times **more**; join with slip st to first dc, finish off: 48 dc and 16 sps.

## SQUARE B (Make 38)

**Rnd 1** (Right side): With White, ch 4, 2 dc in fourth ch from hook, (ch 3, 3 dc in same ch) 3 times, dc in top of beginning ch-4 to form last ch-3 sp: 12 dc and 4 ch-3 sps.

**Note:** Mark Rnd 1 as **right** side.

**Rnd 2:** Ch 1, (sc, ch 7, sc) in last ch-3 sp made, ★ ch 5, (sc, ch 7, sc) in next corner ch-3 sp; repeat from ★ 2 times **more**, ch 2, dc in first sc to form last ch-5 sp: 8 sps.

**Rnd 3:** Ch 3 **(counts as first dc, now and throughout)**, 2 dc in last ch-5 sp made, ch 1, (3 dc, ch 3, 3 dc) in next corner ch-7 sp, ★ ch 1, 3 dc in next ch-5 sp, ch 1, (3 dc, ch 3, 3 dc) in next corner ch-7 sp; repeat from ★ 2 times **more**, sc in first dc to form last ch-1 sp: 36 dc and 12 sps.

*Instructions continued on page 16.*

# DENVER RIPPLE

**MATERIALS**
Bulky Weight Yarn **⑤** BULKY
[6 ounces, 185 yards (170 grams, 169 meters) per skein]:
    Tan - 5 skeins
    Black - 2 skeins
    Variegated - 2 skeins
Crochet hook, size N (9 mm) **or** size needed for gauge

■■□□ **EASY**

**Finished Size:** 40" x 65"
(101.5 cm x 165 cm)

**GAUGE:** In pattern,
        2 repeats and 8 rows = 6" (15.25 cm)

**Gauge Swatch:** 6³/₄"w x 6"h
    (17.25 cm x 15.25 cm)
With Tan, ch 21.
Work same as Afghan Body for 8 rows.
Finish off.

## AFGHAN BODY
With Tan, ch 131.

**Row 1** (Right side): Dc in fourth ch from hook
**(3 skipped chs count as first dc)** and in next 2 chs,
3 dc in next ch, ★ dc in next 3 chs, skip next
3 chs, dc in next 3 chs, 3 dc in next ch; repeat
from ★ across to last 4 chs, dc in last 4 chs:
119 dc.

**Row 2:** Ch 3 **(counts as first dc, now and
throughout)**, turn; skip first 3 dc, (dc, ch 1, dc) in
next dc, [skip next dc, (dc, ch 1, dc) in next dc]
twice, ★ skip next 4 dc, (dc, ch 1, dc) in next dc,
[skip next dc, (dc, ch 1, dc) in next dc] twice;
repeat from ★ across to last 3 dc, skip next 2 dc,
dc in last dc: 80 dc and 39 ch-1 sps.

**Row 3:** Ch 3, turn; dc in next ch-1 sp and in next
2 dc, 3 dc in next ch-1 sp, dc in next 2 dc and in
next ch-1 sp, ★ skip next 2 dc, dc in next ch-1 sp
and in next 2 dc, 3 dc in next ch-1 sp, dc in next
2 dc and in next ch-1 sp; repeat from ★ across to
last 2 dc, skip next dc, dc in last dc; finish off:
119 dc.

**Row 4:** With **right** side facing, join Black with
slip st in first dc; ch 1, sc in same st, ch 1, skip
next 2 dc, sc in next dc, ch 1, skip next dc, (sc,
ch 2, sc) in next dc, ★ ch 1, sc in next dc, ch 1,
skip next dc, sc in next dc, skip next 2 dc, sc in
next dc, ch 1, skip next dc, sc in next dc, ch 1,
(sc, ch 2, sc) in next dc; repeat from ★ across to
last 5 dc, ch 1, skip next dc, sc in next dc, ch 1,
skip next 2 dc, sc in last dc; finish off: 65 sps.

**Row 5:** With **right** side facing, join Variegated with
slip st in first sc; ch 3, dc in next ch-1 sp, 2 dc in
next ch-1 sp, 3 dc in next ch-2 sp, 2 dc in next
ch-1 sp, ★ dc in each of next 2 ch-1 sps, 2 dc in
next ch-1 sp, 3 dc in next ch-2 sp, 2 dc in next
ch-1 sp; repeat from ★ across to last ch-1 sp, dc
in last ch-1 sp and in last sc; finish off: 119 dc.

*Instructions continued on page 16.*

continued from DENVER RIPPLE page 14

**Row 6:** With **right** side facing, join Black with slip st in first dc; ch 1, sc in same st, ch 1, skip next 2 dc, sc in next dc, ch 1, skip next dc, (sc, ch 2, sc) in next dc, ★ ch 1, sc in next dc, ch 1, skip next dc, sc in next dc, skip next 2 dc, sc in next dc, ch 1, skip next dc, sc in next dc, ch 1, (sc, ch 2, sc) in next dc; repeat from ★ across to last 5 dc, ch 1, skip next dc, sc in next dc, ch 1, skip next 2 dc, sc in last dc; finish off: 65 sps.

**Row 7:** With **right** side facing, join Tan with slip st in first sc; ch 3, dc in next ch-1 sp, 2 dc in next ch-1 sp, 3 dc in next ch-2 sp, 2 dc in next ch-1 sp, ★ dc in each of next 2 ch-1 sps, 2 dc in next ch-1 sp, 3 dc in next ch-2 sp, 2 dc in next ch-1 sp; repeat from ★ across to last ch-1 sp, dc in last ch-1 sp and in last sc: 119 dc.

**Rows 8-87:** Repeat Rows 2-7, 13 times; then repeat Rows 2 and 3 once **more**.

*Design by Maggie Weldon.*

continued from GLIMPSE OF GRANNY page 12

**Rnd 4:** Ch 3, 2 dc in last ch-1 sp made, ch 1, 3 dc in next ch-1 sp, ch 1, (3 dc, ch 3, 3 dc) in next corner ch-3 sp, ch 1, ★ (3 dc in next ch-1 sp, ch 1) twice, (3 dc, ch 3, 3 dc) in next corner ch-3 sp, ch 1; repeat from ★ 2 times **more**; join with slip st to first dc, finish off: 48 dc and 16 sps.

## ASSEMBLY

With White and using Placement Diagram as a guide, working through **both** loops on **both** pieces, whipstitch Squares together forming 7 vertical strips of 11 Squares each *(Fig. 9a, page 125)*, beginning in center ch of first corner ch-3 and ending in center ch of next corner ch-3; then whipstitch strips together in same manner.

**PLACEMENT DIAGRAM**

| A | B | A | B | A | B | A |
|---|---|---|---|---|---|---|
| B | A | B | A | B | A | B |
| A | B | A | B | A | B | A |
| B | A | B | A | B | A | B |
| A | B | A | B | A | B | A |
| B | A | B | A | B | A | B |
| A | B | A | B | A | B | A |
| B | A | B | A | B | A | B |
| A | B | A | B | A | B | A |
| B | A | B | A | B | A | B |

## EDGING

**Rnd 1:** With **right** side facing, join White with sc in any corner ch-3 sp *(see Joining With Sc, page 122)*; ch 3, sc in same sp, ★ † ch 1, skip next dc, sc in next dc, ch 1, (sc in next ch-1 sp, ch 1, skip next dc, sc in next dc, ch 1) 3 times, [(sc in next sp, ch 1) twice, skip next dc, sc in next dc, ch 1, (sc in next ch-1 sp, ch 1, skip next dc, sc in next dc, ch 1) 3 times] across to next corner ch-3 sp †, (sc, ch 3, sc) in corner ch-3 sp; repeat from ★ 2 times **more**, then repeat from † to † once; join with slip st to first sc: 324 sps.

**Rnd 2:** Slip st in corner ch-3 sp, ch 1, ★ (sc, ch 3, sc) in corner ch-3 sp, ch 1, (sc in next ch-1 sp, ch 1) across to next corner ch-3 sp; repeat from ★ around; join with slip st to first sc: 328 sps.

**Rnd 3:** (Slip st, ch 3, 2 dc, ch 3, 3 dc) in first corner ch-3 sp, ★ † ch 1, skip next ch-1 sp, (3 dc in next ch-1 sp, ch 1, skip next ch-1 sp) across to next corner ch-3 sp †, (3 dc, ch 3, 3 dc) in corner ch-3 sp; repeat from ★ 2 times **more**, then repeat from † to † once; join with slip st to first dc, finish off: 168 sps.

**Rnd 4:** With **right** side facing, join Green with dc in any corner ch-3 sp; (2 dc, ch 3, 3 dc) in same sp, ch 1, (3 dc in next ch-1 sp, ch 1) across to next corner ch-3 sp, ★ (3 dc, ch 3, 3 dc) in corner ch-3 sp, ch 1, (3 dc in next ch-1 sp, ch 1) across to next corner ch-3 sp; repeat from ★ 2 times **more**; join with slip st to first dc, finish off: 172 sps.

**Rnd 5:** With Purple, repeat Rnd 4: 176 sps.

**Rnd 6:** With Teal, repeat Rnd 4: 180 sps.

**Rnd 7:** With Purple, repeat Rnd 4: 184 sps.

**Rnd 8:** Repeat Rnd 4: 188 sps.

**Rnd 9:** With **right** side facing, join White with dc in any corner ch-3 sp; 2 dc in same sp, ch 1, (3 dc in next ch-1 sp, ch 1) across to next corner ch-3 sp, ★ (3 dc, ch 3, 3 dc) in corner ch-3 sp, ch 1, (3 dc in next ch-1 sp, ch 1) across to next corner ch-3 sp; repeat from ★ 2 times **more**, 3 dc in same sp as first dc, dc in first dc to form last corner ch-3 sp: 192 sps.

**Rnd 10:** Ch 6, dc in third ch from hook, dc in same sp, (ch 3, dc in third ch from hook, dc in same sp) twice, ★ † [dc in next ch-1 sp, (ch 3, dc in third ch from hook, dc in same sp)] across to next corner ch-3 sp †, dc in corner ch-3 sp, (ch 3, dc in third ch from hook, dc in same sp) 3 times; repeat from ★ 2 times **more**, then repeat from † to † once; join with slip st to third ch of beginning ch-6, finish off.

*Design by Anne Halliday.*

# CREATIVE CIRCLES

**MATERIALS**

Medium Weight Yarn 【4】

[3.5 ounces, 216 yards (100 grams, 197 meters) per skein]:
   Brown - 9 skeins
   Scraps - 3 skeins **total**
   **Note:** We used 3 different colors. Refer to page 126 for the list of colors.
Crochet hook, size H (5 mm) **or** size needed for gauge
Safety pin
Yarn needle

■■■□ INTERMEDIATE

**Finished Size:** 46" x 62"
(117 cm x 157.5 cm)

**GAUGE:** Each Motif = 5$^1/_4$" (13.25 cm)
(from straight edge to straight edge)
Each Square = 2$^1/_4$" (5.75 cm)

**Gauge Swatch:** 2$^1/_4$" (5.75 cm)
Work same as Motif through Rnd 2.

## STITCH GUIDE

**TREBLE CROCHET** *(abbreviated tr)*
YO twice, insert hook in dc indicated, YO and pull up a loop (4 loops on hook), (YO and draw through 2 loops on hook) 3 times.

## MOTIF (Make 88)

**Rnd 1** (Right side): With Brown, ch 2, 8 sc in second ch from hook; join with slip st to first sc.

**Note:** Loop a short piece of yarn around any stitch to mark Rnd 1 as **right** side.

**Rnd 2:** Ch 4 **(counts as first dc plus ch 1, now and throughout)**, dc in same st, ch 1, (dc, ch 1) twice in next sc and in each sc around; join with slip st to first dc, place loop from hook onto safety pin to keep piece from unraveling as you work the next rnd: 16 dc and 16 ch-1 sps.

**Rnd 3:** With **wrong** side facing and keeping safety pin and Brown to **wrong** side of work, join Scrap color with sc in any dc **(see Joining With Sc, page 122)**; ch 1, (sc in next dc, ch 1) around; join with slip st to first sc, finish off.

**Rnd 4:** With **right** side facing, remove safety pin and place loop onto hook, ch 2, sc in next sc on Rnd 3, ch 2, (sc in next sc, ch 2) around; skip first ch-2 and join with slip st to first sc, place loop from hook onto safety pin to keep piece from unraveling as you work the next rnd.

*Instructions continued on page 20.*

**Rnd 5:** With **wrong** side facing and keeping safety pin and Brown to **wrong** side of work, join Scrap color with sc in any sc; ch 2, (sc in next sc, ch 2) around; join with slip st to first sc, finish off.

**Rnd 6:** With **right** side facing, remove safety pin and place loop onto hook, ch 2, slip st in next sc on Rnd 5, ch 4, (dc, ch 3, dc) in next sc, ch 1, ★ dc in next sc, ch 1, (dc, ch 3, dc) in next sc, ch 1; repeat from ★ around; skip first ch-2 and join with slip st to first dc, finish off: 24 dc and 8 ch-3 sps.

## SQUARE (Make 70)

**Rnd 1 (Right side):** With Brown, ch 2, (sc, ch 3) 4 times in second ch from hook; join with slip st to first sc: 4 sc and 4 ch-3 sps.

**Note:** Mark Rnd 1 as **right** side.

**Rnd 2:** Ch 3 **(counts as first dc)**, (2 dc, ch 3, 2 dc) in next ch-3 sp, ★ dc in next sc, (2 dc, ch 3, 2 dc) in next ch-3 sp; repeat from ★ 2 times **more**; join with slip st to first dc, finish off: 20 dc and 4 ch-3 sps.

## TRIANGLE (Make 34)

**Row 1:** With Brown, ch 5, (hdc, ch 3, hdc, ch 1, dc) in fifth ch from hook **(4 skipped chs count as first dc plus ch 1)**: 4 sts and 3 sps.

**Row 2 (Right side):** Ch 5 **(counts as first tr plus ch 1)**, turn; 2 dc in next ch-1 sp, dc in next hdc, (2 dc, ch 3, 2 dc) in next ch-3 sp, dc in next hdc, 2 dc in next ch-1 sp, ch 1, tr in last dc; finish off: 12 sts, 2 ch-2 sps, and one corner ch-3 sp.

**Note:** Mark Row 2 as **right** side.

## ASSEMBLY

With Brown, using Placement Diagram as a guide, and working through **both** loops, whipstitch Motifs together **(Fig. 9a, page 125)**, forming 8 vertical strips of 11 Motifs each, beginning in center ch of first corner ch-3 and ending in center ch of next corner ch-3.

Whipstitch 10 Squares to first strip matching center ch of corner ch-3 on Motif to center ch of corner ch-3 on Square; then whipstitch second strip to first strip. Continue joining Squares and strips in same manner.

Whipstitch Triangles to outer edges, beginning in first tr on Triangle and corresponding center ch of corner ch-3 on Motif and ending in last tr on Triangle and corresponding center ch of next corner ch-3 on next Motif.

**PLACEMENT DIAGRAM**

# EDGING

**Rnd 1:** With **right** side facing and working across short edge of Afghan, join Brown with dc in first unworked ch-3 sp on top corner Motif **(see Joining With Dc, page 122)**; ch 3, dc in same sp, ★ † ch 1, (dc in next ch-1 sp, ch 1) twice, (dc, ch 3, dc) in next ch-3 sp, ch 1, (dc in next sp, ch 1) 3 times; working in end of rows across Triangle, sc in first row, ch 1, sc in top of dc on next row, ch 1, sc in free loop of beginning ch **(Fig. 4b, page 123)**, ch 1, sc in top of dc on next row, ch 1, sc in last row, ch 1, ♥ working across next Motif, (dc in next sp, ch 1) 4 times, working in end of rows across Triangle, sc in first row, ch 1, sc in top of dc on next row, ch 1, sc in free loop of beginning ch, ch 1, sc in top of dc on next row, ch 1, sc in last row, ch 1 ♥; repeat from ♥ to ♥ across to last Motif, working across last Motif, (dc in next sp, ch 1) 3 times †, (dc, ch 3, dc) in next ch-3 sp; repeat from ★ 2 times **more**, then repeat from † to † once; join with slip st to first dc: 374 sps.

**Rnd 2:** Ch 1, (sc, ch 1) twice in first ch-3 sp, ★ (sc in next ch-1 sp, ch 1) across to next ch-3 sp, (sc, ch 1, sc) in next ch-3 sp, place marker around ch-1 just made for st placement, ch 1; repeat from ★ 6 times **more**, (sc in next ch-1 sp, ch 1) across; join with slip st to first sc, finish off.

**Rnd 3:** With **wrong** side facing, join Scrap color with sc in ch-1 sp before joining; ch 1, ★ (sc in next ch-1 sp, ch 1) across to next marked ch-1 sp, sc in marked ch-1 sp, remove marker and place around sc just made for st placement; repeat from ★ 6 times **more**, (sc in next ch-1 sp, ch 1) across; join with slip st to first sc, finish off.

**Rnd 4:** With **right** side facing, join Brown with sc in same st as joining; ch 1, ★ (sc in next ch-1 sp, ch 1) across to next marked sc, sc in marked sc, remove marker and place around sc just made for st placement; repeat from ★ 6 times **more**, (sc in next ch-1 sp, ch 1) across; join with slip st to first sc, finish off: 382 ch-1 sps.

**Rnd 5:** With **wrong** side facing, join Scrap color with sc in ch-1 sp before joining; ch 1, ★ (sc in next ch-1 sp, ch 1) across to next marked sc, remove marker and place around last ch-1 made for st placement; repeat from ★ 6 times **more**, (sc in next ch-1 sp, ch 1) across; join with slip st to first sc, finish off.

**Rnd 6:** With **right** side facing, join Brown with sc in ch-1 sp before joining; ch 1, ★ (sc in next ch-1 sp, ch 1) across to next marked ch-1 sp, sc in marked ch-1 sp, remove marker and place around sc just made for st placement, ch 1; repeat from ★ 6 times **more**, (sc in next ch-1 sp, ch 1) across; join with slip st to first sc, finish off.

**Rnd 7:** With **wrong** side facing, join Scrap color with sc in same st as joining; ch 1, ★ (sc in next ch-1 sp, ch 1) across to next marked sc, sc in marked sc, remove marker; repeat from ★ 6 times **more**, (sc in next ch-1 sp, ch 1) across; join with slip st to first sc, finish off: 390 ch-1 sps.

**Rnd 8:** With **right** side facing, join Brown with sc in sc in any ch-1 sp; ch 1, (sc in next ch-1 sp, ch 1) around; join with slip st to first sc, do **not** finish off.

**Rnd 9:** Slip st in first ch-1 sp, ch 1, (slip st in next ch-1 sp, ch 1) around; join with slip st to first slip st, finish off.

*Design by Anne Halliday.*

# TILE

**MATERIALS**
Medium Weight Yarn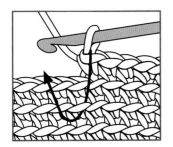
[3.5 ounces, 216 yards (100 grams, 197 meters) per skein]:
  Taupe - 13 skeins
  Natural - 11 skeins
Crochet hook, size H (5 mm) **or** size needed for gauge

**INTERMEDIATE**

**Finished Size:** 50" x 70"
(127 cm x 178 cm)

**GAUGE:** In pattern, 15 sts = 4" (10 cm)

## STITCH GUIDE

**LONG DOUBLE CROCHET** *(abbreviated Ldc)*
YO, insert hook from **top** to **bottom** in free loop of st one row **below** st indicated *(Fig. A)*, YO and pull up a loop (3 loops on hook), (YO and draw through 2 loops on hook) twice. Skip st behind Ldc.

**Fig. A**

Each row is worked across length of Afghan with **right** side facing throughout. When joining yarn and finishing off, leave a 6" (15 cm) end to be worked into fringe.

## AFGHAN
With Taupe, ch 264.

**Row 1** (Right side)**:** Sc in second ch from hook and in each ch across; finish off: 263 sc.

***Note:*** Loop a short piece of yarn around any stitch to mark Row 1 as **right** side.

**Row 2:** With **right** side facing, join Natural with sc in **both** loops of first sc *(see Joining With Sc, page 122)*; sc in BLO of next sc *(Fig. 2, page 123)* and each sc across to last sc, sc in **both** loops of last sc; finish off.

**Row 3:** With **right** side facing, join Taupe with sc in **both** loops of first sc; sc in BLO of next 3 sts, (work Ldc in next 3 sts, sc in BLO of next 3 sts) across to last sc, sc in **both** loops of last sc; finish off: 134 sc and 129 Ldc.

**Row 4:** With **right** side facing, join Natural with sc in **both** loops of first sc; work Ldc in next st, sc in BLO of next st, work Ldc in next st, ★ sc in BLO of next 3 sts, work Ldc in next st, sc in BLO of next st, work Ldc in next st; repeat from ★ across to last sc, sc in **both** loops of last sc; finish off: 175 sc and 88 Ldc.

*Instructions continued on page 27.*

# COMFY

**MATERIALS**
Medium Weight Yarn 🔵 **4**
[5 ounces, 275 yards (140 grams, 251 meters) per skein]:
 Blue - 9 skeins
 Lt Blue - 8 skeins
Crochet hook, size I (5.5 mm) **or** size needed for gauge
Safety pins - 2

◼◼◼◻ **INTERMEDIATE**

**Finished Size:** 47½" x 67½"
(120.5 cm x 171.5 cm)

**GAUGE:** In pattern,
  (2 dc, ch 3) 4 times = 4½" (11.5 cm);
  14 rows = 4¼" (10.75 cm)

**Gauge Swatch:** 5½"w x 4¼"h (14 cm x 10.75 cm)
With Blue, ch 30; place marker in eighth ch from hook for st placement.
Work same as Afghan for 14 rows.
Finish off both colors.

Afghan consists of two intertwined layers, with each layer being a different color. After the first two rows form a foundation, these colors are worked alternately, with each row of a particular color being crocheted into the stitches or spaces on the last row of that same color. Each row is worked across the length of the Afghan.

At the end of each row, slip the loop from the crochet hook onto a safety pin as instructed; this will keep the piece from unraveling while working the next row. At the end of each Lt Blue row, drop yarn to the side of the Afghan specified in instructions; this placement is necessary for the yarn to be in the correct position for working the next Lt Blue row. Yarn at the end of each Blue row may be dropped to either side.

## AFGHAN

With Blue, ch 305; place marker in eighth ch from hook for st placement.

**Row 1** (Right side): Working in back ridge of chs **(Fig. 1, page 122)**, dc in tenth ch from hook and in next ch, ch 3, ★ skip next 3 chs, dc in next 2 chs, ch 3; repeat from ★ across to last 4 chs, skip next 3 chs, dc in last ch; slip loop from hook onto safety pin: 119 dc and 60 sps.

**Note:** Loop a short piece of yarn around any stitch to mark Row 1 as **right** side.

**Row 2:** With **right** side facing, working in back ridge of skipped chs on beginning ch and in **front** of last row **(Fig. 7, page 124)**, join Lt Blue with dc in marked ch **(see Joining With Dc, page 122)**; ch 3, working **behind** last row, dc in same ch as last dc made, ★ working in **front** of last row, dc in center ch of next ch-3, ch 3, working **behind** last row, dc in same ch as last dc made; repeat from ★ across; slip loop from hook onto safety pin and drop Lt Blue to **back** of work, slip Blue loop from safety pin onto hook: 120 dc and 60 ch-3 sps.

*Instructions continued on page 26.*

**Row 3:** Ch 6 **(counts as first dc plus ch 3, now and throughout)**, turn; working in dc on previous Blue row and keeping last Lt Blue row to back of work, (dc in next 2 dc, ch 3) across, dc in last sp on previous Blue row; slip loop from hook onto safety pin.

**Row 4:** With **wrong** side facing and keeping loop in **front** of last Blue row, slip Lt Blue loop from safety pin onto hook, ch 6, working **behind** last Blue row, dc in first ch-3 sp on previous Lt Blue row, ★ working in **front** of last Blue row, dc in next ch-3 sp on previous Lt Blue row, ch 3, working **behind** last Blue row, dc in same sp on previous Lt Blue row; repeat from ★ across; slip loop from hook onto safety pin and drop Lt Blue to **back** of work, slip Blue loop from safety pin onto hook.

**Row 5:** Ch 6, turn; working in dc on previous Blue row and keeping last Lt Blue row to back of work, (dc in next 2 dc, ch 3) across to last ch-3 sp, dc in last ch-3 sp; slip loop from hook onto safety pin.

**Row 6:** With **right** side facing and keeping loop in **front** of last Blue row, slip Lt Blue loop from safety pin onto hook, ch 6, working **behind** last Blue row, dc in first ch-3 sp on previous Lt Blue row, ★ working in **front** of last Blue row, dc in next ch-3 sp on previous Lt Blue row, ch 3, working **behind** last Blue row, dc in same sp on previous Lt Blue row; repeat from ★ across; slip loop from hook onto safety pin and drop Lt Blue to **back** of work, slip Blue loop from safety pin onto hook.

**Row 7:** Ch 6, turn; working in dc on previous Blue row and keeping last Lt Blue row to back of work, (dc in next 2 dc, ch 3) across to last ch-3 sp, dc in last ch-3 sp; slip loop from hook onto safety pin.

Repeat Rows 4-7 for pattern until Afghan measures approximately 47" (119.5 cm) from beginning ch, ending by working Row 7.

**Next Row:** With **wrong** side facing and keeping loop in **front** of last Blue row, slip Lt Blue loop from safety pin onto hook, ch 6, working **behind** last Blue row, dc in first ch-3 sp on previous Lt Blue row, ★ working in **front** of last Blue row, dc in next ch-3 sp on previous Lt Blue row, ch 3, working **behind** last Blue row, dc in same sp on previous Lt Blue row; repeat from ★ across; finish off Lt Blue, slip Blue loop from safety pin onto hook.

**Last Row:** Ch 1, turn; working **behind** last Lt Blue row, sc in first dc on previous Blue row, ch 3, working in dc on previous Blue row and keeping last Lt Blue row to back of work, (sc in next 2 dc, ch 3) across to last ch-3 sp, sc in last ch-3 sp; finish off.

Holding 4 strands of Blue together, each 19" (48.5 cm) long, add fringe across short edges of Afghan **(Figs. 10a & b, page 125)**, working through one loop of each color for each fringe.

*Design by Melissa Leapman.*

continued from TILE page 22

**Row 5:** With **right** side facing, join Taupe with sc in **both** loops of first sc; sc in BLO of next 3 sts, (work Ldc in next 3 sts, sc in BLO of next 3 sts) across to last sc, sc in **both** loops of last sc; finish off: 134 sc and 129 Ldc.

**Row 6:** With **right** side facing, join Natural with sc in **both** loops of first sc; sc in BLO of next sc and each sc across to last sc, sc in **both** loops of last sc; finish off: 263 sc.

**Row 7:** With **right** side facing, join Taupe with sc in **both** loops of first sc; work Ldc in next 3 sts, (sc in BLO of next 3 sts, work Ldc in next 3 sts) across to last sc, sc in **both** loops of last sc; finish off: 131 sc and 132 Ldc.

**Row 8:** With **right** side facing, join Natural with sc in **both** loops of first sc; sc in BLO of next 3 sts, ★ work Ldc in next st, sc in BLO of next st, work Ldc in next st, sc in BLO of next 3 sts; repeat from ★ across to last sc, sc in **both** loops of last sc; finish off: 177 sc and 86 Ldc.

**Row 9:** With **right** side facing, join Taupe with sc in **both** loops of first sc; work Ldc in next 3 sts, (sc in BLO of next 3 sts, work Ldc in next 3 sts) across to last sc, sc in **both** loops of last sc; finish off: 131 sc and 132 Ldc.

**Row 10:** With **right** side facing, join Natural with sc in **both** loops of first sc; sc in BLO of next st and each st across to last sc, sc in **both** loops of last sc; finish off: 263 sc.

Repeat Rows 3-10 for pattern until Afghan measures approximately 50" (127 cm) from beginning ch, ending by working Row 5.

**Last Row:** With **right** side facing and working in both loops across entire row, join Taupe with sc in first sc; sc in each st across; finish off.

Holding 2 strands of each color together, each 12" (30.5 cm) long, add additional fringe in every other row across short edges of Afghan *(Figs. 10a & b, page 125)*.

*Design by Melissa Leapman.*

# TINY TWIRLS

## MATERIALS

Medium Weight Yarn **[4]**
[7 ounces, 364 yards (198 grams, 333 meters) per skein]:
   Ecru - 4 skeins
   Purple - 1 skein
   Pink - 1 skein
   Yellow - 1 skein
   Green - 1 skein
Crochet hook, size I (5.5 mm) **or** size needed for gauge
Safety pin
Yarn needle

**INTERMEDIATE**

**Finished Size:** 34$^1/_2$" x 45"
(87.5 cm x 114.5 cm)

---

**GAUGE SWATCH:** 3$^1/_2$" (9 cm) square
Work same as Square.

## STITCH GUIDE

**TREBLE CROCHET** *(abbreviated tr)*
YO twice, insert hook in st or sp indicated, YO and pull up a loop (4 loops on hook), (YO and draw through 2 loops on hook) 3 times.

**FRONT POST TREBLE CROCHET** *(abbreviated FPtr)*
YO twice, insert hook from **front** to **back** around post of dc indicated *(Fig. 5, page 124)*, YO and pull up a loop (4 loops on hook), (YO and draw through 2 loops on hook) 3 times. Skip st behind FPtr.

## SQUARE (Make 108)

Working Rnd 3 with Purple, Pink, Yellow, or Green, make 27 Squares with **each** color.

**Rnd 1** (Right side)**:** With Ecru, ch 2, 8 sc in second ch from hook; join with slip st to first sc.

**Note:** Loop a short piece of yarn around any stitch to mark Rnd 1 as **right** side.

**Rnd 2:** Ch 4 **(counts as first dc plus ch 1, now and throughout)**, dc in same st, ch 1, (dc, ch 1) twice in next sc and in each sc around; join with slip st to first dc; place loop from hook onto safety pin to keep piece from unraveling as you work the next rnd: 16 dc and 16 ch-1 sps.

**Rnd 3:** With **right** side facing and keeping safety pin and working yarn on **wrong** side of work, join color indicated with slip st around post of last dc made *(Fig. 5, page 124)*; ch 5 **(counts as first FPtr plus ch 1)**, work FPtr around next dc, place marker around last ch made for st placement, ch 1, (FPtr around next dc, ch 1) around; join with slip st to first FPtr, finish off.

**Rnd 4:** With **right** side facing, remove safety pin and place Ecru loop onto hook, ch 1, working **behind** sts on Rnd 3 *(Fig. 7, page 124)*, sc in next ch-1 sp on Rnd 2, sc in marked sp on Rnd 3, remove marker, (sc in next ch-1 sp on Rnd 2, sc in next ch-1 sp on Rnd 3) around; join with slip st to first sc: 32 sc.

**Rnd 5:** Ch 4, ★ † skip next sc, sc in next sc, ch 1, skip next sc, slip st in next sc, ch 1, skip next sc, sc in next sc, ch 1, skip next sc †, (dc, ch 3, dc) in next sc, ch 1; repeat from ★ 2 times **more**, then repeat from † to † once, dc in same st as first dc, ch 3; join with slip st to first dc, finish off: 20 sts and 20 sps.

*Instructions continued on page 33.*

# BLUE LACE

**MATERIALS**  MEDIUM **4**                    ▬▬▭ **INTERMEDIATE**
Medium Weight Yarn
[3.5 ounces, 205 yards (100 grams, 187 meters) per skein]:
  18 skeins
Crochet hook, size H (5 mm) **or** size needed for gauge

**Finished Size:** 51$\frac{1}{2}$" x 68"
(131 cm x 172.5 cm)

**GAUGE:** In pattern, one repeat = 5$\frac{1}{4}$" (13.25 cm)
        and 8 rows = 4" (10 cm)

**Gauge Swatch:** 7"w x 4"h (17.75 cm x 10 cm)
Ch 26.
Work same as Afghan Body for 8 rows.
Finish off.

## STITCH GUIDE

### FRONT POST DOUBLE CROCHET
### *(abbreviated FPdc)*
YO, insert hook from **front** to **back** around post
of st indicated *(Fig. 5, page 124)*, YO and pull
up a loop (3 loops on hook), (YO and draw
through 2 loops on hook) twice.

### BACK POST DOUBLE CROCHET *(abbreviated BPdc)*
YO, insert hook from **back** to **front** around post
of st indicated *(Fig. 5, page 124)*, YO and pull
up a loop (3 loops on hook), (YO and draw
through 2 loops on hook) twice.

### V-STITCH *(abbreviated V-St)*
(Dc, ch 3, dc) in st or sp indicated.

### PICOT
Ch 3, sc in third ch from hook.

## AFGHAN BODY

Ch 145; place marker in third ch from hook for st
placement.

**Row 1:** Work V-St in sixth ch from hook **(5 skipped
chs count as first dc plus 2 skipped chs)**, ★ skip
next 2 chs, dc in next 2 chs, (ch 2, skip next
ch, sc in next ch, ch 2, skip next ch, dc in next
2 chs) twice, skip next 2 chs, work V-St in next
ch; repeat from ★ across to last 3 chs, skip next
2 chs, dc in last ch: 84 sts and 41 sps.

**Row 2** (Right side): Ch 3 **(counts as first dc, now
and throughout)**, turn; work FPdc around next dc,
3 dc in next ch-3 sp, ★ work FPdc around next
2 dc, work V-St in next dc, skip next 2 ch-2 sps,
work V-St in next 2 dc, skip next 2 ch-2 sps, work
V-St in next dc, work FPdc around next 2 dc, 3 dc
in next ch-3 sp; repeat from ★ across to last 2 dc,
work FPdc around next dc, dc in last dc: 127 sts
and 32 ch-3 sps.

**Row 3:** Ch 3, turn; skip next FPdc and next dc,
work V-St in next dc, ★ skip next dc and next
FPdc, work BPdc around next FPdc, dc in next
dc, ch 2, skip next ch-3 sp, sc in sp **between** next
2 dc *(Fig. 8, page 124)*, ch 2, skip next ch-3 sp,
dc in next 2 dc, ch 2, skip next ch-3 sp, sc in sp
**between** next 2 dc, ch 2, skip next ch-3 sp, dc in
next dc, work BPdc around next FPdc, skip next
FPdc and next dc, work V-St in next dc; repeat
from ★ across to last 3 sts, skip next dc and next
FPdc, dc in last dc: 84 sts and 41 sps.

*Instructions continued on page 32.*

**Row 4:** Ch 3, turn; work FPdc around next dc, 3 dc in next ch-3 sp, ★ work FPdc around next 2 sts, work V-St in next dc, skip next 2 ch-2 sps, work V-St in next 2 dc, skip next 2 ch-2 sps, work V-St in next dc, work FPdc around next 2 sts, 3 dc in next ch-3 sp; repeat from ★ across to last 2 dc, work FPdc around next dc, dc in last dc: 127 sts and 32 ch-3 sps.

Repeat Rows 3 and 4 until Afghan Body measures approximately 60" (152.5 cm) from beginning ch, ending by working Row 4, do **not** finish off.

## EDGING

**Rnd 1:** Ch 6 **(counts as first dc plus ch 3, now and throughout)**, do **not** turn; dc in last dc made, working across end of rows, skip first row, (work V-St around dc at end of next row, skip next row) across to marked ch on last row, dc in marked ch, (ch 3, dc in same ch) 3 times; working in free loops of beginning ch **(Fig. 4b, page 123)**, skip next 2 chs, work V-St in next ch, † skip next 5 chs, work V-St in next ch, skip next 2 chs, work V-St in next ch, skip next ch, work V-St in next ch, skip next 5 chs, work V-St in next ch †; repeat from † to † across to last 3 chs, skip next 2 chs, dc in last ch, (ch 3, dc in same ch) 3 times; working across end of rows, skip first 2 rows, (work V-St around dc at end of next row, skip next row) across; working across last row, dc in first dc, (ch 3, dc in same st) 3 times, skip next 2 sts, work V-St in next dc, ★ skip next 4 sts, work V-St in next ch-3 sp, skip next ch-3 sp, work V-St in sp **between** next 2 dc, skip next ch-3 sp, work V-St in next ch-3 sp, skip next 4 sts, work V-St in next dc; repeat from ★ across to last 2 sts, skip last 2 sts, (dc, ch 3, dc) in same st as first dc, ch 1, hdc in first dc to form last ch-3 sp.

**Rnd 2:** Ch 2 **(counts as first hdc)**, turn; 2 hdc in last ch-3 sp made, 5 hdc in next ch-3 sp and in each ch-3 sp around, 2 hdc in same sp as first hdc; join with slip st to first hdc.

**Rnd 3:** Ch 6, turn; dc in same st, ★ skip next 4 hdc, (work V-St in next hdc, skip next 4 hdc) across to center hdc of next corner 5-hdc group, dc in corner hdc, (ch 3, dc in same st) 3 times; repeat from ★ 2 times **more**, skip next 4 hdc, (work V-St in next hdc, skip next 4 hdc) across, (dc, ch 3, dc) in same st as first dc, ch 1, hdc in first dc to form last ch-3 sp.

**Rnds 4-6:** Repeat Rnds 2 and 3 once, then repeat Rnd 2 once **more**.

**Rnd 7:** Ch 1, turn; working in Back Loops Only **(Fig. 2, page 123)**, (sc, work Picot, sc) in same st, sc in next 4 hdc, ★ (sc, work Picot, sc) in next hdc, sc in next 4 hdc; repeat from ★ around; join with slip st to first sc, finish off.

*Design by Barbara Shaffer.*

## ASSEMBLY

With Ecru, using Placement Diagram as a guide and working through **both** loops of **both** pieces, whipstitch Squares together forming 9 vertical strips of 12 Squares each **(Fig. 9a, page 125)**, beginning in center ch of first corner ch-3 and ending in center ch of next corner ch-3; then whipstitch strips together in same manner.

### PLACEMENT DIAGRAM

| A | B | A | B | A | B | A | B | A |
|---|---|---|---|---|---|---|---|---|
| C | D | C | D | C | D | C | D | C |
| B | A | B | A | B | A | B | A | B |
| D | C | D | C | D | C | D | C | D |
| A | B | A | B | A | B | A | B | A |
| C | D | C | D | C | D | C | D | C |
| B | A | B | A | B | A | B | A | B |
| D | C | D | C | D | C | D | C | D |
| A | B | A | B | A | B | A | B | A |
| C | D | C | D | C | D | C | D | C |
| B | A | B | A | B | A | B | A | B |
| D | C | D | C | D | C | D | C | D |

**KEY**
**A - Purple**  **B - Pink**  **C - Yellow**  **D - Green**

## EDGING

**Rnd 1:** With **right** side facing, join Ecru with sc in any corner ch-3 sp **(see Joining With Sc, page 122)**; ch 3, sc in same sp, ch 1, (sc in next sp, ch 1) across to next corner ch-3 sp, ★ (sc, ch 3, sc) in corner ch-3 sp, ch 1, (sc in next sp, ch 1) across to next corner ch-3 sp; repeat from ★ 2 times **more**; join with slip st to first sc: 252 sc and 252 sps.

**Rnd 2:** Ch 1, turn; ★ (sc in next ch-1 sp, ch 1) across to next corner ch-3 sp, (sc, ch 3, sc) in corner ch-3 sp, ch 1; repeat from ★ around; join with slip st to first sc, finish off: 260 sc and 260 sps.

**Rnd 3:** With **right** side facing, working in **front** of Rnd 2 and in sc and corner ch-3 sps on Rnd 1, join Pink with slip st in first corner ch-3 sp (between sc); ch 5, † (tr in next sc, ch 1) across to next corner ch-3 sp, tr in corner ch-3 sp †, ch 2, cut Pink; with Yellow, ch 1, tr in same sp, ch 1; repeat from † to † once, ch 2, cut Yellow; with Green, ch 1, tr in same sp, ch 1; repeat from † to † once, ch 2, cut Green; with Purple, ch 1, tr in same sp, ch 1; repeat from † to † once, ch 3; join with slip st to first tr, finish off.

**Rnd 4:** With **right** side facing, join Ecru with sc in any corner ch-3 sp; working **behind** Rnd 3, sc in ch-1 sp after corner ch-3 sp on Rnd 2, ★ † sc in same corner ch-3 sp on Rnd 3, (sc in next ch-1 sp on Rnd 2, sc in next ch-1 sp on Rnd 3) across to within 2 ch-1 sps of next corner ch-3 sp on Rnd 3, sc in next corner ch-3 sp on Rnd 2, sc in next ch-1 sp on Rnd 3, sc in same corner ch-3 sp on Rnd 2, sc in next ch-1 sp on Rnd 3, place marker in last sc made for st placement, sc in same corner ch-3 sp on Rnd 2 †, sc in next corner ch-3 sp on Rnd 3, sc in next ch-1 sp on Rnd 2; repeat from ★ 2 times **more**, then repeat from † to † once; join with slip st to first sc.

**Rnd 5:** Ch 1, sc in same st, ch 1, skip next sc, ★ (sc in next sc, ch 1, skip next sc) across to marked sc, (sc, ch 1) twice in marked sc, remove marker, skip next sc; repeat from ★ 3 times **more**, sc in next sc, ch 1; join with slip st to first sc.

**Rnd 6:** (Slip st in next ch-1 sp, ch 1) around; join with slip st to first slip st, finish off.

*Design by Anne Halliday.*

# GREEK KEY

## MATERIALS

MEDIUM 4

Medium Weight Yarn
[5 ounces, 256 yards (140 grams, 234 meters) per skein]:
   Gold - 9 skeins
   Brown - 8 skeins
Crochet hook, size H (5 mm) **or** size needed for gauge

INTERMEDIATE

**Finished Size:** 47" x 68"
(119 cm x 173 cm)

**GAUGE:** In pattern, 14 sts = 4" (10 cm)

## STITCH GUIDE

**LONG DOUBLE CROCHET (abbreviated Ldc)**
YO, insert hook from **top** to **bottom** in free loop of st 2 rows **below** st indicated **(Fig. A)**, YO and pull up a loop (3 loops on hook), (YO and draw through 2 loops on hook) twice. Skip st behind Ldc.

**Fig. A**

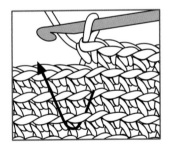

## AFGHAN

With Gold, ch 167.

**Row 1 (Right side):** Sc in second ch from hook and in each ch across: 166 sc.

**Note:** Loop a short piece of yarn around any stitch to mark Row 1 as **right** side.

**To change color**, work last sc until 2 loops remain on hook, drop old yarn, with new color **(Fig. 3a, page 123)**, YO and draw through both loops on hook. Carry dropped color loosely along edge of Afghan until needed again.

**Row 2:** Ch 1, turn; sc in each sc across changing to Brown in last sc made.

**Row 3:** Ch 1, turn; sc in **both** loops first sc, sc in BLO of next sc **(Fig. 2, page 123)** and each sc across to last sc, sc in **both** loops of last sc.

**Row 4:** Ch 1, turn; sc in both loops of each sc across changing to Gold in last sc made.

**Row 5:** Ch 1, turn; sc in **both** loops of first sc, sc in BLO of next sc, work Ldc in next st, (sc in BLO of next 5 sc, work Ldc in next st) across to last sc, sc in **both** loops of last sc: 138 sc and 28 Ldc.

**Row 6:** Ch 1, turn; sc in both loops of each sc across changing to Brown in last sc made: 166 sc.

**Row 7:** Ch 1, turn; sc in **both** loops of first sc, sc in BLO of next 2 sc, ★ work Ldc in next st, sc in BLO of next 3 sc, work Ldc in next st, sc in BLO of next sc; repeat from ★ across to last sc, sc in **both** loops of last sc: 112 sc and 54 Ldc.

**Row 8:** Ch 1, turn; sc in both loops of each sc across changing to Gold in last sc made.

*Instructions continued on page 39.*

# EXCEPTIONAL

## MATERIALS

Medium Weight Yarn **④** MEDIUM **4**
[3.5 ounces, 208 yards (100 grams, 190 meters) per skein]:
  Brown - 8 skeins
  Maroon - 3 skeins
  Dk Brown - 3 skeins
  Cream - 2 skeins
Crochet hook, size J (6 mm) **or** size needed for gauge

■■■□ INTERMEDIATE

**Finished Size:** 51" x 69"
(129.5 cm x 175.5 cm)

**GAUGE:** In pattern, 2 repeats = $7^1/_2$" (19 cm);
     8 rows = $4^1/_4$" (10.75 cm)

**Gauge Swatch:** $7^1/_2$"w x $5^1/_2$"h (19 cm x 14 cm)
With Brown, ch 30.
Work same as Afghan Body Rows 1-8.

## STITCH GUIDE

**FRONT POST TREBLE CROCHET** *(abbreviated FPtr)*
YO twice, insert hook from **front** to **back**
around post of dc indicated *(Fig. 5, page 124)*,
YO and pull up a loop (4 loops on hook), (YO
and draw through 2 loops on hook) 3 times.
**PICOT**
Ch 3, sc in third ch from hook.

## AFGHAN BODY

With Brown, ch 206.

**Row 1** (Right side): Sc in second ch from hook
and in next 5 chs, 3 sc in next ch, sc in next
6 chs, ★ skip next 3 chs, sc in next 6 chs, 3 sc in
next ch, sc in next 6 chs; repeat from ★ across:
195 sc.

**Note:** Loop a short piece of yarn around any stitch
to mark Row 1 as **right** side.

**Row 2:** Ch 1, turn; skip first sc, working in both
loops, hdc in next 6 sc, 3 hdc in next sc, hdc
in next 6 sc, ★ skip next 2 sc, hdc in next 6 sc,
3 hdc in next sc, hdc in next 6 sc; repeat from
★ across to last sc, leave last sc unworked:
195 hdc.

**Row 3:** Ch 1, turn; skip first hdc, working in BLO
*(Fig. 2, page 123)*, sc in next 6 hdc, 3 sc in next
hdc, sc in next 6 hdc, ★ skip next 2 hdc, sc in
next 6 hdc, 3 sc in next hdc, sc in next 6 hdc;
repeat from ★ across to last hdc, leave last hdc
unworked.

**Row 4:** Ch 2, turn; skip first 2 sc, working in both
loops, (dc, ch 1, dc) in next sc, skip next 2 sc,
(dc, ch 1, dc) in next sc, [skip next sc, (dc, ch 1,
dc) in next sc] twice, skip next 2 sc, (dc, ch 1,
dc) in next sc, ★ skip next 4 sc, (dc, ch 1, dc) in
next sc, skip next 2 sc, (dc, ch 1, dc) in next sc,
[skip next sc, (dc, ch 1, dc) in next sc] twice, skip
next 2 sc, (dc, ch 1, dc) in next sc; repeat from
★ across to last 2 sc, skip next sc, hdc in last sc;
finish off.

*Instructions continued on page 38.*

**Row 5:** With **right** side facing, skip first hdc and join Maroon with sc in next dc *(see Joining With Sc, page 122)*; work 2 FPtr around next dc, sc in next ch, work 2 FPtr around next dc, 3 dc in next ch-1 sp, (skip next dc, work 2 FPtr around next dc, sc in next ch) twice, ★ skip next 2 dc, (sc in next ch, work 2 FPtr around next dc) twice, 3 dc in next ch-1 sp, (skip next dc, work 2 FPtr around next dc, sc in next ch) twice; repeat from ★ across to last 2 sts, leave last 2 sts unworked; finish off.

**Row 6:** With **wrong** side facing, skip first sc and join Dk Brown with sc in next FPtr; sc in next 5 sts, 3 sc in next dc, sc in next 6 sts, ★ skip next 2 sc, sc in next 6 sts, 3 sc in next dc, sc in next 6 sts; repeat from ★ across to last sc, leave last sc unworked; finish off.

**Row 7:** With **right** side facing and working in BLO, skip first sc and join Cream with sc in next sc; sc in next 5 sc, 3 sc in next sc, sc in next 6 sc, ★ skip next 2 sc, sc in next 6 sc, 3 sc in next sc, sc in next 6 sc; repeat from ★ across to last sc, leave last sc unworked; finish off.

**Row 8:** With **wrong** side facing and working in BLO, skip first sc and join Dk Brown with sc in next sc; sc in next 5 sc, 3 sc in next sc, sc in next 6 sc, ★ skip next 2 sc, sc in next 6 sc, 3 sc in next sc, sc in next 6 sc; repeat from ★ across to last sc, leave last sc unworked; finish off.

**Row 9:** With **right** side facing and working in BLO, skip first sc and join Brown with sc in next sc; sc in next 5 sc, 3 sc in next sc, sc in next 6 sc, ★ skip next 2 sc, sc in next 6 sc, 3 sc in next sc, sc in next 6 sc; repeat from ★ across to last sc, leave last sc unworked; do **not** finish off.

Repeat Rows 2-9 for pattern until Aghan Body measures approximately 67" (170 cm) from beginning ch, ending by working Row 3, do **not** finish off.

## EDGING

Ch 3, turn; skip first 2 sc, working in both loops, (dc, work Picot, dc) in next sc, skip next 2 sc, (dc, work Picot, dc) in next sc, skip next sc, (dc, work 2 Picots, dc) in next sc, skip next sc, (dc, work Picot, dc) in next sc, skip next 2 sc, (dc, work Picot, dc) in next sc, ★ skip next 4 sc, (dc, work Picot, dc) in next sc, skip next 2 sc, (dc, work Picot, dc) in next sc, skip next sc, (dc, work 2 Picots, dc) in next sc, skip next sc, (dc, work Picot, dc) in next sc, skip next 2 sc, (dc, work Picot, dc) in next sc; repeat from ★ across to last 2 sc, skip next sc, (dc, work 2 Picots, dc) in last sc; working in top of sts at end of rows, [(dc, work Picot, dc) in next row, skip next row] across; working in free loops of beginning ch *(Fig. 4b, page 123)*, (dc, work 2 Picots, dc) in ch at base of first sc, [skip next ch, (dc, work Picot, dc) in next ch] twice, † skip next 3 chs, [(dc, work Picot, dc) in next ch, skip next 2 chs] twice, (dc, work 2 Picots, dc) in next ch, [skip next 2 chs, (dc, work Picot, dc) in next ch] twice †; repeat from † to † across to last 8 chs, skip next 3 chs, [(dc, work Picot, dc) in next ch, skip next ch] twice, (dc, work 2 Picots, dc) in last ch; working in top of sts at end of rows, skip first row, (dc, work Picot, dc) in next row, [skip next row, (dc, work Picot, dc) in next row] across; dc in same st as beginning ch-3, work 2 Picots; join with slip st to third ch of beginning ch-3, finish off.

*Design by Barbara Shaffer.*

**Row 9:** Ch 1, turn; sc in **both** loops of first sc, sc in BLO of next sc, work Ldc in next st, ★ sc in BLO of next 3 sc, work Ldc in next st, sc in BLO of next sc, work Ldc in next st; repeat from ★ across to last sc, sc in **both** loops of last sc: 111 sc and 55 Ldc.

**Row 10:** Ch 1, turn; sc in both loops of each sc across changing to Brown in last sc made: 166 sc.

**Row 11:** Ch 1, turn; sc in **both** loops of first sc, work Ldc in next st, (sc in BLO of next 5 sc, work Ldc in next st) across to last 2 sc, sc in BLO of next sc, sc in **both** loops of last sc: 138 sc and 28 Ldc.

**Row 12:** Ch 1, turn; sc in both loops of each sc across changing to Gold in last sc made: 166 sc.

**Row 13:** Ch 1, turn; sc in **both** loops of first sc, sc in BLO of next sc and and each sc across to last sc, sc in **both** loops of last sc.

**Row 14:** Ch 1, turn; sc in both loops of each sc across changing to Brown in last sc made.

**Row 15:** Ch 1, turn; sc in **both** loops of first sc, sc in BLO of next 4 sc, work Ldc in next st, (sc in BLO of next 5 sc, work Ldc in next st) across to last 4 sc, sc in BLO of next 3 sc, sc in **both** loops of last sc: 139 sc and 27 Ldc.

**Row 16:** Ch 1, turn; sc in both loops of each sc across changing to Gold in last sc made: 166 sc.

**Row 17:** Ch 1, turn; sc in **both** loops of first sc, ★ sc in BLO of next 3 sc, work Ldc in next st, sc in BLO of next sc, work Ldc in next st; repeat from ★ across to last 3 sc, sc in BLO of next 2 sc, sc in **both** loops of last sc: 112 sc and 54 Ldc.

**Row 18:** Ch 1, turn; sc in both loops of each sc across changing to Brown in last sc made: 166 sc.

**Row 19:** Ch 1, turn; sc in **both** loops of first sc, sc in BLO of next 2 sc, ★ work Ldc in next st, sc in BLO of next sc, work Ldc in next st, sc in BLO of next 3 sc; repeat from ★ across to last sc, sc in **both** loops of last sc: 112 and 54 Ldc.

**Row 20:** Ch 1, turn; sc in both loops of each sc across changing to Gold in last sc made: 166 sc.

**Row 21:** Ch 1, turn; sc in **both** loops of first sc, sc in BLO of next 3 sc, work Ldc in next st, (sc in BLO of next 5 sc, work Ldc in next st) across to last 5 sc, sc in BLO of next 4 sc, sc in **both** loops of last sc: 139 sc and 27 Ldc.

**Row 22:** Ch 1, turn; sc in both loops of each sc across changing to Brown in last sc made: 166 sc.

**Row 23:** Ch 1, turn; sc in **both** loops of first sc, sc in BLO of next sc and and each sc across to last sc, sc in **both** loops of last sc.

Repeat Rows 4-23 for pattern until Afghan measures approximately 68" (172.5 cm) from beginning ch, ending by working Row 22; at end of last row, do **not** change to Brown, cut Brown and finish off Gold.

## SIDE EDGING (Optional)
With **right** side facing and working in end of rows, join Gold with sc in first row (**see Joining With Sc, page 122**); sc in each row across; finish off.

Repeat across opposite side.

Holding 7 strands of Gold together, each 12" (30.5 cm) long, add fringe evenly spaced across short edges (about 6 sts apart) (**Figs. 10a & b, page 125**).

*Design by Melissa Leapman.*

# CHARMING

**MATERIALS**

Medium Weight Yarn [MEDIUM 4]

[5 ounces, 256 yards (140 grams, 234 meters) per skein]:
   10 skeins
Crochet hook, size H (5 mm) **or** size needed for gauge

■■■◻ **INTERMEDIATE**

**Finished Size:** 50¹⁄₂" x 69"
(128.5 cm x 175.5 cm)

**GAUGE:** Each Strip = 7"w (17.75 cm)

**Gauge Swatch:** 1¹⁄₄"w x 9"h (3.25 cm x 22.75 cm)
**Foundation:** Ch 7; join with slip st to form a ring,
ch 6, dc in third ch from hook to form a ring,
ch 7, tr in fourth ch from hook to form a ring,
ch 6, dc in third ch from hook to form a ring,
ch 10, slip st in seventh ch from hook to form last
ring: 5 rings.
**Rnd 1:** Being careful not to twist Foundation,
slip st in next 3 chs and in next ring, ch 5 **(counts
as first dc plus ch 2)**, dc in same ring, ch 2, 5 dc
in next ring, ch 2, (dc, ch 2) twice in next ring,
12 dc in last ring, ch 2; working across opposite
side of Foundation, (dc, ch 2) twice in next ring,
5 dc in next ring, ch 2, (dc, ch 2) twice in next
ring, 12 dc in last ring, ch 2; join with slip st to
first dc, finish off.

## STITCH GUIDE

**TREBLE CROCHET** *(abbreviated tr)*
YO twice, insert hook in st or sp indicated, YO
and pull up a loop (4 loops on hook), (YO and
draw through 2 loops on hook) 3 times.

**POPCORN**
4 Dc in sc indicated, drop loop from hook,
insert hook in first dc of 4-dc group, hook
dropped loop and draw through st *(Fig. 6,
page 124)*.

**DECREASE**
Pull up a loop in each of next 2 ch-2 sps, YO
and draw through all 3 loops on hook.

**JOINING DECREASE**
Pull up a loop in sp **before** joining and in sp
**after** joining, YO and draw through all 3 loops
on hook.

**PICOT**
Ch 2, slip st in top of last sc made.

## FIRST STRIP
### CENTER

**Foundation:** Ch 7; join with slip st to form a ring,
ch 6, dc in third ch from hook to form a ring,
★ ch 7, tr in fourth ch from hook to form a ring,
ch 6, dc in third ch from hook to form a ring;
repeat from ★ 12 times **more**, ch 10, slip st in
seventh ch from hook to form last ring: 29 rings.

*Instructions continued on page 42.*

**Rnd 1** (Right side): Being careful not to twist Foundation, slip st in next 3 chs and in next ring, ch 5 **(counts as first dc plus ch 2, now and throughout)**, dc in same ring, ch 2, [5 dc in next ring, ch 2, (dc, ch 2) twice in next ring] across to last ring, 12 dc in last ring, ch 2; working across opposite side of Foundation, (dc, ch 2) twice in next ring, [5 dc in next ring, ch 2, (dc, ch 2) twice in next ring] across to last ring, 12 dc in last ring, ch 2; join with slip st to first dc: 210 dc and 84 ch-2 sps.

**Note:** Loop a short piece of yarn around any dc of last 12-dc group made to mark **right** side and bottom edge.

**Rnd 2:** Slip st in first ch-2 sp, ch 5, (dc, ch 2) twice in same sp, † ★ skip next ch-2 sp, (sc in next dc, ch 2) 5 times, skip next ch-2 sp, (dc, ch 2) 3 times in next ch-2 sp; repeat from ★ 12 times **more**, skip next ch-2 sp, (sc in next dc, ch 2) 12 times, skip next ch-2 sp †, (dc, ch 2) 3 times in next ch-2 sp, repeat from † to † once; join with slip st to first dc: 238 ch-2 sps.

**Rnd 3:** (Slip st, ch 5, dc) in first ch-2 sp, ch 2, (dc, ch 2) twice in next ch-2 sp, † ★ skip next ch-2 sp, (sc in next ch-2 sp, ch 2) 4 times, skip next ch-2 sp, (dc, ch 2) twice in each of next 2 ch-2 sps; repeat from ★ 12 times **more**, skip next ch-2 sp, (sc in next ch-2 sp, ch 2) 11 times, skip next ch-2 sp †, (dc, ch 2) twice in each of next 2 ch-2 sps, repeat from † to † once; join with slip st to first dc.

**Rnd 4:** (Slip st, ch 5, dc) in first ch-2 sp, † ch 3, sc in next ch-2 sp, ch 3, (dc, ch 2) twice in next ch-2 sp, ★ skip next ch-2 sp, (sc in next ch-2 sp, ch 2) 3 times, skip next ch-2 sp, (dc, ch 2, dc) in next ch-2 sp, ch 3, sc in next ch-2 sp, ch 3, (dc, ch 2) twice in next ch-2 sp; repeat from ★ 12 times **more**, skip next ch-2 sp, (sc in next ch-2 sp, ch 2) 10 times, skip next ch-2 sp †, (dc, ch 2, dc) in next ch-2 sp, repeat from † to † once; join with slip st to first dc.

**Rnd 5:** (Slip st, ch 5, dc) in first ch-2 sp, † ch 3, sc in next ch-3 sp, work Popcorn in next sc, sc in next ch-3 sp, ch 3, (dc, ch 2) twice in next ch-2 sp, ★ skip next ch-2 sp, (sc in next ch-2 sp, ch 2) twice, skip next ch-2 sp, (dc, ch 2, dc) in next ch-2 sp, ch 3, sc in next ch-3 sp, work Popcorn in next sc, sc in next ch-3 sp, ch 3, (dc, ch 2) twice in next ch-2 sp; repeat from ★ 12 times **more**, skip next ch-2 sp, (sc in next ch-2 sp, ch 2) 9 times, skip next ch-2 sp †, (dc, ch 2, dc) in next ch-2 sp, repeat from † to † once; join with slip st to first dc: 210 sps.

**Rnd 6:** (Slip st, ch 5, dc) in first ch-2 sp, † ch 3, sc in next ch-3 sp, ch 5, sc in next ch-3 sp, ch 3, ★ (dc, ch 2, dc) in next ch-2 sp, skip next ch-2 sp, dc in next ch-2 sp, skip next ch-2 sp, (dc, ch 2, dc) in next ch-2 sp, ch 3, sc in next ch-3 sp, ch 5, sc in next ch-3 sp, ch 3; repeat from ★ 12 times **more**, (dc, ch 2) twice in next ch-2 sp, skip next ch-2 sp, (sc in next ch-2 sp, ch 2) 8 times, skip next ch-2 sp †, (dc, ch 2, dc) in next ch-2 sp, repeat from † to † once; join with slip st to first dc: 158 sps.

**Rnd 7:** (Slip st, ch 5, dc) in first ch-2 sp, ch 5, (sc in next sp, ch 5) 3 times, [decrease, ch 5, (sc in next sp, ch 5) 3 times] 13 times, place marker around last ch-5 made for joining, (dc, ch 2) twice in next ch-2 sp, skip next ch-2 sp, (sc in next ch-2 sp, ch 2) 7 times, skip next ch-2 sp, (dc, ch 2, dc) in next ch-2 sp, place marker around last ch-2 made for st placement, ch 5, (sc in next sp, ch 5) 3 times, [decrease, ch 5, (sc in next sp, ch 5) 3 times] 13 times, (dc, ch 2) twice in next ch-2 sp, skip next ch-2 sp, (sc in next ch-2 sp, ch 2) 7 times, skip next ch-2 sp; join with slip st to first dc, do **not** finish off.

## BOTTOM POINT
Begin working in rows.

**Row 1:** Slip st in next ch and in same ch-2 sp, ch 5, **turn**; dc in same sp, ch 2, skip next ch-2 sp, (sc in next ch-2 sp, ch 2) 6 times, skip next ch-2 sp, (dc, ch 2, dc) in next ch-2 sp, leave remaining sps unworked: 9 ch-2 sps.

**Rows 2-5:** Turn; (slip st, ch 5, dc) in first ch-2 sp, ch 2, skip next ch-2 sp, (sc in next ch-2 sp, ch 2) across to last 2 ch-2 sps, skip next ch-2 sp, (dc, ch 2, dc) in last ch-2 sp: 5 ch-2 sps.

**Row 6:** Turn; (slip st, ch 5, dc) in first ch-2 sp, skip next ch-2 sp, tr in next ch-2 sp, skip next ch-2 sp, (dc, ch 2, dc) in last ch-2 sp: 2 ch-2 sps.

**Row 7:** Turn; slip st in first ch-2 sp, ch 1, sc in same sp and in last ch-2 sp; finish off: 2 sc.

## TOP POINT

**Row 1:** With **wrong** side facing and working on opposite end of Strip, join yarn with slip st in marked ch-2 sp; ch 5, dc in same sp, ch 2, skip next ch-2 sp, (sc in next ch-2 sp, ch 2) 6 times, skip next ch-2 sp, (dc, ch 2, dc) in next ch-2 sp, leave remaining sps unworked: 9 ch-2 sps.

**Rows 2-7:** Work same as Bottom Point: 2 sc.

## REMAINING 6 STRIPS

Work same as First Strip through Rnd 6 of Center: 158 sps.

**Rnd 7** (Joining rnd): (Slip st, ch 5, dc) in first ch-2 sp, ch 5, (sc in next sp, ch 5) 3 times, [decrease, ch 5, (sc in next sp, ch 5) 3 times] 13 times, place marker around last ch-5 made for joining, (dc, ch 2) twice in next ch-2 sp, skip next ch-2 sp, (sc in next ch-2 sp, ch 2) 7 times, skip next ch-2 sp, (dc, ch 2, dc) in next ch-2 sp, place marker around last ch-2 made for st placement, ch 2; holding Strips with **wrong** sides together and bottom edges at same end, slip st in marked ch-5 sp on **adjacent Strip**, ch 2, (sc in next sp on **new Strip**, ch 2, slip st in next ch-5 sp on **adjacent Strip**, ch 2) 3 times, ★ decrease on **new Strip**, ch 2, slip st in next ch-5 sp on **adjacent Strip**, ch 2, (sc in next sp on **new Strip**, ch 2, slip st in next ch-5 sp on **adjacent Strip**, ch 2) 3 times; repeat from ★ 12 times **more**, (dc, ch 2) twice in next ch-2 sp on **new Strip**, skip next ch-2 sp, (sc in next ch-2 sp, ch 2) 7 times, skip next ch-2 sp; join with slip st to first dc, do **not** finish off.

## BOTTOM AND TOP POINTS

Work same as Bottom and Top Points of First Strip; at end of Top Point on Seventh Strip, do **not** finish off.

## EDGING

Ch 1, turn; sc in first sc, † ch 4, slip st in third ch from hook, ch 1, sc in next sc, (3 sc, work Picot) in end of next 6 rows, sc in sp **before** next dc on Strip Center, ★ work joining decrease, sc in sp **after** next dc on Strip Center, (work Picot, 3 sc) in end of next 6 rows, sc in next sc, ch 4, slip st in third ch from hook, ch 1, sc in next sc, (3 sc, work Picot) in end of next 6 rows, sc in sp **before** next dc on Strip Center; repeat from ★ 5 times **more**, (3 sc in next ch-5 sp, work Picot) 56 times, sc in sp **after** next dc on Strip Center, 3 sc in end of next row, (work Picot, 3 sc) in end of next 5 rows †, sc in next sc, repeat from † to † once; join with slip st to first sc, finish off.

*Design by Patricia Kristoffersen.*

# November

**MATERIALS**
Medium Weight Yarn
[7 ounces, 364 yards (198 grams, 333 meters) per skein]:
   10 skeins
Crochet hook, size J (6 mm) **or** size needed for gauge

**INTERMEDIATE**

**Finished Size:** 54" x 73"
(137 cm x 185.5 cm)

**GAUGE:** 11 dc and 8 rows = 4" (10 cm)

**Gauge Swatch:** 4" (10 cm) square
Ch 13.
**Row 1:** Dc in fourth ch from hook **(3 skipped chs count as first dc)** and in each ch across: 11 dc.
**Rows 2-8:** Ch 3 **(counts as first dc)**, turn; dc in next dc and in each dc across.
Finish off.

## STITCH GUIDE

### FRONT POST DOUBLE CROCHET
**(abbreviated FPdc)**
YO, insert hook from **front** to **back** around post of st indicated **(Fig. 5, page 124)**, YO and pull up a loop even with loop on hook (3 loops on hook), (YO and draw through 2 loops on hook) twice.

### BACK POST DOUBLE CROCHET
**(abbreviated BPdc)**
YO, insert hook from **back** to **front** around post of st indicated **(Fig. 5, page 124)**, YO and pull up a loop even with loop on hook (3 loops on hook), (YO and draw through 2 loops on hook) twice.

### POPCORN (uses one dc)
4 Dc in dc indicated, drop loop from hook, insert hook in first dc of 4-dc group, hook dropped loop and draw through st **(Fig. 6, page 124)**.

### CABLE (uses next 4 sts)
Skip next 2 sts, work FPdc around each of next 2 sts, work FPdc around second skipped st, work FPdc around first skipped st.

### SHELL (uses one st or sp)
2 Dc in st or sp indicated, (ch 1, 2 dc in same st or sp) twice.

*Instructions continued on page 46.*

## AFGHAN BODY

Ch 136; place marker in third ch from hook for Edging placement.

**Row 1:** Dc in fourth ch from hook **(3 skipped chs count as first dc)** and in each ch across: 134 dc.

**Row 2** (Right side)**:** Ch 3 **(counts as first dc, now and throughout)**, turn; ★ † work FPdc around next dc, (dc in next dc, work FPdc around next dc) twice, dc in next 2 dc, work Popcorn in next dc, dc in next 2 dc, work FPdc around next dc, dc in next 2 dc, work Cable, dc in next 2 dc, work FPdc around next dc, dc in next 2 dc, work Popcorn in next dc, dc in next 2 dc †, work FPdc around next dc, (dc in next dc, work FPdc around next dc) twice, dc in next 5 dc, work FPdc around next dc, dc in next dc, skip next 3 dc, work Shell in next dc, skip next 3 dc, dc in next dc, work FPdc around next dc, dc in next 5 dc; repeat from ★ once **more**, then repeat from † to † once, (work FPdc around next dc, dc in next dc) 3 times: 132 sts and 4 ch-1 sps.

**Row 3:** Ch 3, turn; ★ † work BPdc around next FPdc, (dc in next dc, work BPdc around next FPdc) twice, dc in next 5 sts, work BPdc around next FPdc, dc in next 2 dc, work BPdc around each of next 4 FPdc, dc in next 2 dc, work BPdc around next FPdc, dc in next 5 sts †, work BPdc around next FPdc, (dc in next dc, work BPdc around next FPdc) twice, dc in next 5 dc, work BPdc around next FPdc, dc in next dc, ch 2, (sc in next ch-1 sp, ch 2) twice, skip next 2 dc, dc in next dc, work BPdc around next FPdc, dc in next 5 dc; repeat from ★ once **more**, then repeat from † to † once, (work BPdc around next FPdc, dc in next dc) 3 times: 124 sts and 6 ch-2 sps.

**Row 4:** Ch 3, turn; ★ † (work FPdc around next BPdc, dc in next dc) 3 times, (work Popcorn in next dc, dc in next dc) twice, work FPdc around next BPdc, dc in next 2 dc, work FPdc around each of next 4 BPdc, dc in next 2 dc, work FPdc around next BPdc, (dc in next dc, work Popcorn in next dc) twice, (dc in next dc, work FPdc around next BPdc) 3 times †, dc in next 5 dc, work FPdc around next BPdc, dc in next dc, skip next ch-2 sp, work Shell in next ch-2 sp, skip next ch-2 sp, dc in next dc, work FPdc around next BPdc, dc in next 5 dc; repeat from ★ once **more**, then repeat from † to † once, dc in last dc: 132 sts and 4 ch-1 sps.

**Row 5:** Ch 3, turn; ★ † work BPdc around next FPdc, (dc in next dc, work BPdc around next FPdc) twice, dc in next 5 sts, work BPdc around next FPdc, dc in next 2 dc, work BPdc around each of next 4 FPdc, dc in next 2 dc, work BPdc around next FPdc, dc in next 5 sts †, work BPdc around next FPdc, (dc in next dc, work BPdc around next FPdc) twice, dc in next 5 dc, work BPdc around next FPdc, dc in next dc, ch 2, (sc in next ch-1 sp, ch 2) twice, skip next 2 dc, dc in next dc, work BPdc around next FPdc, dc in next 5 dc; repeat from ★ once **more**, then repeat from † to † once, (work BPdc around next FPdc, dc in next dc) 3 times: 124 sts and 6 ch-2 sps.

**Row 6:** Ch 3, turn; ★ † work FPdc around next BPdc, (dc in next dc, work FPdc around next BPdc) twice, dc in next 2 dc, work Popcorn in next dc, dc in next 2 dc, work FPdc around next dc, dc in next 2 dc, work Cable, dc in next 2 dc, work FPdc around next BPdc, dc in next 2 dc, work Popcorn in next dc, dc in next 2 dc †, work FPdc around next BPdc, (dc in next dc, work FPdc around next BPdc) twice, dc in next 5 dc, work FPdc around next BPdc, dc in next dc, skip next ch-2 sp, work Shell in next ch-2 sp, skip next ch-2 sp, dc in next dc, work FPdc around next BPdc, dc in next 5 dc; repeat from ★ once **more**, then repeat from † to † once, (work FPdc around next BPdc, dc in next dc) 3 times: 132 sts and 4 ch-1 sps.

**Row 7:** Repeat Row 5.

**Row 8:** Ch 3, turn; ★ † work FPdc around next BPdc, (dc in next dc, work FPdc around next BPdc) twice, dc in next 5 dc, work FPdc around next BPdc, dc in next 2 dc, work FPdc around each of next 4 BPdc, dc in next 2 dc, work FPdc around next BPdc, dc in next 5 dc †, work FPdc around next BPdc, (dc in next dc, work FPdc around next BPdc) twice, dc in next 5 dc, work FPdc around next BPdc, dc in next dc, skip next ch-2 sp, work Shell in next ch-2 sp, skip next ch-2 sp, dc in next dc, work FPdc around next BPdc, dc in next 5 dc; repeat from ★ once **more**, then repeat from † to † once, (work FPdc around next BPdc, dc in next dc) 3 times: 132 sts and 4 ch-1 sps.

**Rows 9 and 10:** Repeat Rows 5 and 6.

Repeat Rows 3-10 for pattern until Afghan Body measures approximately 67$\frac{1}{2}$" (171.5 cm) from beginning ch, ending by working Row 7; do **not** finish off.

# EDGING

**Rnd 1:** Ch 3, turn; 4 dc in same st, ★ dc in each st across to next ch-2 sp, 2 dc in next ch-2 sp, dc in next sc, dc in next ch-2 sp and in next sc, 2 dc in next ch-2 sp; repeat from ★ once **more**, dc in each st across to last dc, 5 dc in last dc; work 182 dc evenly spaced across end of rows; working in free loops of beginning ch *(Fig. 4b, page 123)*, 5 dc in marked ch, dc in next ch and in each ch across to last ch, 5 dc in last ch; work 182 dc evenly spaced across end of rows; join with slip st to first dc: 648 dc.

**Rnd 2:** (Slip st, ch 3, dc) in next dc, (ch 1, 2 dc in same st) twice, skip next dc, work Shell in next dc, ★ (skip next 4 dc, work Shell in next dc) across to center dc of next corner 5-dc group, skip center dc, work Shell in next dc; repeat from ★ 2 times **more**, skip next 4 dc, (work Shell in next dc, skip next 4 dc) across; join with slip st to first dc: 132 Shells.

**Rnd 3:** Slip st in next dc and in next ch-1 sp, ch 1, sc in same sp, ch 2, sc in next ch-1 sp, ch 4, ★ sc in next ch-1 sp, ch 2, sc in next ch-1 sp, ch 4; repeat from ★ around; join with slip st to first sc: 264 sps.

**Rnd 4:** Slip st in first ch-2 sp, ch 3, (dc, ch 1, 2 dc) in same sp, sc in next ch-4 sp, (work Shell in next ch-2 sp, sc in next ch-4 sp) around, 2 dc in same sp as first dc, sc in first dc to form last ch-1 sp: 132 sc and 132 Shells.

**Rnd 5:** Ch 1, sc in last ch-1 sp made, ch 2, sc in next ch-1 sp, † ch 4, skip next 2 dc, sc in next sc, ch 4, (sc in next ch-1 sp, ch 2, sc in next ch-1 sp, ch 4) 28 times, skip next 2 dc, sc in next sc †, (ch 4, sc in next ch-1 sp, ch 2, sc in next ch-1 sp) 38 times, repeat from † to † once, (ch 4, sc in next ch-1 sp, ch 2, sc in next ch-1 sp) across, ch 1, dc in first sc to form last ch-4 sp: 268 sps.

**Rnd 6:** Ch 1, (sc, ch 3, sc) in last ch-4 sp made and in each sp around; join with slip st to first sc, finish off.

*Design by Barbara Shaffer.*

# OCTOBER

**MATERIALS**

Medium Weight Yarn [4]
[7 ounces, 364 yards (198 grams, 333 meters) per skein]:
  11 skeins
Crochet hook, size J (6 mm) **or** size needed for gauge

◼◼◼◻ **INTERMEDIATE**

**Finished Size:** 52" x 62"
(132 cm x 157.5 cm)

**GAUGE:** In pattern, 20 sts = 6³/₄" (17.25 cm);
         10 rows = 4" (10 cm)

**Gauge Swatch:** 6¹/₄"w x 4"h (16 cm x 10 cm)
Ch 21.
Work same as Afghan Body for 10 rows.
Finish off.

## STITCH GUIDE

### FRONT POST DOUBLE CROCHET
### (abbreviated FPdc)

YO, insert hook from **front** to **back** around post of st indicated **(Fig. 5, page 124)**, YO and pull up a loop even with loop on hook (3 loops on hook), (YO and draw through 2 loops on hook) twice.

### CABLE (uses next 3 FPdc)

Skip next FPdc in row **below** next sc, work FPdc around each of next 2 FPdc, working in **front** of FPdc just made, work FPdc around skipped FPdc. Skip 3 sc behind Cable.

### CLUSTER (uses one sc)

★ YO, insert hook in sc indicated, YO and pull up a loop, YO and draw through 2 loops on hook; repeat from ★ 5 times **more**, YO and draw through all 7 loops on hook.

## AFGHAN BODY

Ch 151; place marker in third ch from hook for Edging placement.

**Row 1** (Right side)**:** Dc in fourth ch from hook **(3 skipped chs count as first dc)** and in each ch across: 149 dc.

**Row 2:** Ch 1, turn; sc in each dc across.

**Row 3:** Ch 3 **(counts as first dc, now and throughout)**, turn; dc in next 2 sc, skip dc in row **below** next sc, work FPdc around each of next 2 dc, working in **front** of FPdc just made, work FPdc around skipped dc, skip 3 sc behind FPdc, dc in next 3 sc, ★ work Cluster in next sc, dc in next 3 sc, skip dc in row **below** next sc, work FPdc around each of next 2 dc, working in **front** of FPdc just made, work FPdc around skipped dc, skip 3 sc behind FPdc, dc in next 3 sc; repeat from ★ across: 45 FPdc and 14 Clusters.

**Row 4:** Ch 1, turn; sc in each st across: 149 sc.

*Instructions continued on page 55.*

# JAZZY JOURNEY

**MATERIALS**

Bulky Weight Yarn **5** BULKY
[3 ounces, 135 yards (85 grams, 123 meters) per skein]:
    Lt Green - 8 skeins
    Green - 7 skeins
Crochet hook, size K (6.5 mm) **or** size needed for gauge

◼◼◻◻ **EASY**

**Finished Size:** 45" x 57"
(114.5 cm x 145 cm)

**GAUGE:** In pattern,
        one repeat (18 sts) = 6" (15.25 cm);
        20 rows = 6³/₄" (17.25 cm)

**Gauge Swatch:** 9"w x 6³/₄"h
    (22.75 cm x 17.25 cm)
With Lt Green, ch 28.
Work same as Afghan Body for 20 rows.

Each row is worked across length of Afghan. When joining yarn and finishing off, leave an 8" (20.5 cm) end to be worked into fringe.

## AFGHAN BODY
With Lt Green, ch 172.

**Row 1** (Right side): Sc in second ch from hook, ★ ch 1, skip next ch, sc in next ch; repeat from ★ across; finish off: 86 sc and 85 ch-1 sps.

**Note:** Loop a short piece of yarn around any stitch to mark Row 1 as **right** side.

**Row 2:** With **wrong** side facing, join Green with sc in first sc (**see Joining With Sc, page 122**); (ch 1, sc in next sc) 4 times, ★ sc in next ch-1 sp, (ch 1, sc in next ch-1 sp) 4 times, sc in next sc, (ch 1, sc in next sc) 4 times; repeat from ★ across; finish off: 95 sc and 76 ch-1 sps.

**Row 3:** With **right** side facing, join Lt Green with sc in first sc; (ch 1, sc in next sc) 4 times, ★ ch 1, (sc in next ch-1 sp, ch 1) 4 times, skip next sc, sc in next sc, (ch 1, sc in next sc) 4 times; repeat from ★ across; finish off: 86 sc and 85 ch-1 sps.

**Row 4:** With **wrong** side facing, join Green with sc in first sc; (ch 1, sc in next sc) 4 times, ★ sc in next ch-1 sp, (ch 1, sc in next ch-1 sp) 4 times, sc in next sc, (ch 1, sc in next sc) 4 times; repeat from ★ across; finish off: 95 sc and 76 ch-1 sps.

**Rows 5-12:** Repeat Rows 3 and 4, 4 times.

**Row 13:** With **right** side facing, join Lt Green with sc in first sc; sc in next ch-1 sp, (ch 1, sc in next ch-1 sp) 3 times, ★ ch 1, skip next sc, sc in next sc, (ch 1, sc in next sc) 4 times, (ch 1, sc in next ch-1 sp) 4 times; repeat from ★ across to last sc, sc in last sc; finish off: 87 sc and 84 ch-1 sps.

**Row 14:** With **wrong** side facing, join Green with sc in first sc; ★ (ch 1, sc in next ch-1 sp) 4 times, sc in next sc, (ch 1, sc in next sc) 4 times, sc in next ch-1 sp; repeat from ★ across to last 3 ch-1 sps, (ch 1, sc in next ch-1 sp) 3 times, ch 1, skip next sc, sc in last sc; finish off: 95 sc and 76 ch-1 sps.

**Rows 15-22:** Repeat Rows 13 and 14, 4 times.

*Instructions continued on page 55.*

# SPRING SERENADE

**MATERIALS**
Medium Weight Yarn (4)
[5 ounces, 256 yards (140 grams, 234 meters) per skein]:
  White - 8 skeins
  Teal - 3 skeins
Crochet hook, size I (5.5 mm) **or** size needed for gauge
Yarn needle

**INTERMEDIATE**

**Finished Size:** 50" x 68"
(127 cm x 172.5 cm)

**GAUGE:** In pattern,
  (Cluster, ring) 3 times = 4$\frac{1}{2}$" (11.5 cm)
  Each Strip = 4$\frac{1}{2}$" (11.5 cm) wide

**Gauge Swatch:** 4$\frac{1}{2}$"w x 9$\frac{1}{2}$"h
      (11.5 cm x 24.25 cm)
**Foundation Row** (Right side): With White, ch 3, dc in third ch from hook (ring made), ★ work Cluster, ch 3, dc in third ch from hook; repeat from ★ 2 times **more**, ch 1; finish off: 3 Clusters and 4 rings.
**Rnds 1-3:** Work same as Strip.

## STITCH GUIDE

### TREBLE CROCHET (abbreviated tr)
YO twice, insert hook in sp indicated, YO and pull up a loop (4 loops on hook), (YO and draw through 2 loops on hook) 3 times.

### CLUSTER
Ch 3, YO, insert hook in third ch from hook, YO and pull up a loop, YO and draw through 2 loops on hook, YO, insert hook in same ch, YO and pull up a loop, YO and draw through 2 loops on hook, YO and draw through all 3 loops on hook.

### SHELL
(2 Dc, ch 2, 2 dc) in sp indicated.
**DECREASE** (uses next 2 dc)
YO, † insert hook in **next** dc, YO and pull up a loop, YO and draw through 2 loops on hook †, YO, skip next joining, repeat from † to † once, YO and draw through all 3 loops on hook.

## STRIP (Make 11)
### CENTER
**Foundation Row** (Right side): With White, ch 3, dc in third ch from hook (ring made), ★ work Cluster, ch 3, dc in third ch from hook; repeat from ★ 40 times **more**, ch 1; finish off: 41 Clusters and 42 rings.

**Note:** Loop a short piece of yarn around first Cluster worked to mark **right** side and **bottom** edge.

**Rnd 1:** With **right** side facing, join Teal with dc in last ring made (*see Joining With Dc, page 122*); (dc, ch 2, 2 dc, ch 3, work Shell) in same ring, ch 1, † skip next Cluster, ★ work Shell in next ring, ch 1, skip next Cluster; repeat from ★ across to last ring †, work (Shell, ch 3, Shell) in last ring, ch 1; working on opposite edge of Foundation Row, repeat from † to † once; join with slip st to first dc, finish off: 84 Shells.

*Instructions continued on page 54.*

**Rnd 2:** With **right** side facing, join White with dc in ch-3 sp at bottom edge of Strip; 2 dc in same sp, ch 1, † work Shell in next Shell (ch-2 sp), (tr in next ch-1 sp, work Shell in next Shell) across to next ch-3 sp, ch 1 †, (3 dc, ch 3, 3 dc) in ch-3 sp, ch 1, repeat from † to † once, 3 dc in same sp as first dc, dc in first dc to form last ch-3 sp.

**Rnd 3:** Ch 3 **(counts as first dc)**, (2 dc, ch 3, 3 dc) in last ch-3 sp made, † ch 1, (2 dc in next sp, ch 1) twice, place marker in last ch-1 made for joining, 2 dc in same sp, ch 2, (3 dc in next Shell, ch 2) across to last Shell on same side, 2 dc in last Shell, ch 1, place marker in last ch-1 made for joining, 2 dc in same sp, ch 1, 2 dc in next ch-1 sp, ch 1 †, (3 dc, ch 3, 3 dc) in next ch-3 sp, repeat from † to † once; join with slip st to first dc, finish off: 276 dc and 96 sps.

## ASSEMBLY

Remove markers as Strips are joined leaving markers on outer Strips for Edging placement.

Hold two Strips together with bottom edges at the same end. With White and working through **both** loops of **both** pieces, whipstitch Strips together **(Fig. 9a, page 125)**, beginning and ending in marked ch.

Join remaining Strips in same manner.

## EDGING

With **right** side facing, join White with sc in ch-1 sp after marked ch-1 on top edge **(see Joining With Sc, page 122)**; † ch 1, (dc, ch 1) 3 times in next ch-1 sp, skip next 2 dc, sc in next dc, ch 1, (dc, ch 1) 3 times in next ch-3 sp, sc in next dc, ch 1, (dc, ch 1) 3 times in next ch-1 sp, sc in next ch-1 sp, ★ skip next dc, decrease, sc in next ch-1 sp, ch 1, (dc, ch 1) 3 times in next ch-1 sp, skip next 2 dc, sc in next dc, ch 1, (dc, ch 1) 3 times in next ch-3 sp, sc in next dc, ch 1, (dc, ch 1) 3 times in next ch-1 sp, sc in next ch-1 sp; repeat from ★ across to within 2 dc of next marker, ch 1, skip next 2 dc, (dc, ch 1) 3 times in marked sp, remove marker, sc in next ch-2 sp, [skip next dc, dc in next dc, (ch 1, dc in same st) twice, sc in next ch-2 sp] across to within 2 dc of next marker, ch 1, skip next 2 dc, (dc, ch 1) 3 times in marked sp, remove marker †, sc in next ch-1 sp, repeat from † to † once; join with slip st to first sc, finish off.

*Design by Anne Halliday.*

continued from OCTOBER page 48

**Row 5:** Ch 3, turn; dc in next 2 sc, work Cable, ★ dc in next 2 sc, work Cluster in next sc, dc in next sc, work Cluster in next sc, dc in next 2 sc, work Cable; repeat from ★ across to last 3 sc, dc in last 3 sc: 15 Cables and 28 Clusters.

**Row 6:** Ch 1, turn; sc in each st across: 149 sc.

**Row 7:** Ch 3, turn; dc in next 2 sc, work Cable, dc in next 3 sc, ★ work Cluster in next sc, dc in next 3 sc, work Cable, dc in next 3 sc; repeat from ★ across: 15 Cables and 14 Clusters.

Repeat Rows 4-7 for pattern until Afghan Body measures approximately 60$\frac{1}{2}$" (153.5 cm) from beginning ch, ending by working Row 7; do **not** finish off.

## EDGING

**Rnd 1:** Ch 1, turn; 2 sc in first dc, sc in next dc and in each st across to last dc, (2 sc, ch 1, 2 sc) in last dc; work 216 sc evenly spaced across end of rows; working in free loops of beginning ch **(Fig. 4b, page 123)**, (2 sc, ch 1, 2 sc) in marked ch, sc in next ch and in each ch across to last ch, (2 sc, ch 1, 2 sc) in last ch; work 216 sc evenly spaced across end of rows; 2 sc in same st as first sc, ch 1; join with slip st to first sc: 742 sc and 4 ch-1 sps.

**Rnd 2:** Turn; slip st in first ch-1 sp, ch 3, (dc, ch 1, 2 dc) in same sp, work Cluster in next sc, ★ (dc in next 2 sc, work Cluster in next sc) across to next corner ch-1 sp, (2 dc, ch 1, 2 dc) in corner ch-1 sp, work Cluster in next sc; repeat from ★ 2 times **more**, (dc in next 2 sc, work Cluster in next sc) across; join with slip st to first dc, finish off.

*Design by Jean Kanable.*

continued from JAZZY JOURNEY page 50

**Rows 23-132:** Repeat Rows 3-22, 5 times; then repeat Rows 3-12 once **more**.

**Row 133:** With **right** side facing, join Lt Green with sc in first sc; (ch 1, sc in next sc) 4 times, ★ ch 1, (sc in next ch-1 sp, ch 1) 4 times, skip next sc, sc in next sc, (ch 1, sc in next sc) 4 times; repeat from ★ across; finish off: 86 sc and 85 ch-1 sps.

## TRIM
### FIRST SIDE

With **right** side facing, join Lt Green with slip st in first sc on Row 133; slip st in next ch-1 sp, (ch 1, slip st in next ch-1 sp) across to last sc, slip st in last sc; finish off.

### SECOND SIDE

With **right** side facing and working in free loops **(Fig. 4b, page 123)** and in sps across beginning ch, join Lt Green with slip st in first ch; slip st in next sp, (ch 1, slip st in next sp) across to ch at base of last sc, slip st in ch at base of last sc; finish off.

Holding 2 strands of corresponding color yarn together, each 17" (43 cm) long, add additional fringe in each row across short edges of Afghan **(Figs. 10a & b, page 125)**.

*Design by Anne Halliday.*

# APRIL

**MATERIALS**
Bulky Weight Yarn **[BULKY 5]**
[5 ounces, 255 yards (140 grams, 233 meters) per skein]:
  Blue - 5 skeins
  Variegated - 2 skeins
Crochet hook, size N (9 mm) **or** size needed for gauge
Yarn needle

■■□□ EASY

**Finished Size:** 47¹/₂" x 63"
(120.5 cm x 160 cm)

**GAUGE:** In pattern,
      9 sts and 8 rows = 4¹/₂" (11.5 cm)

**Gauge Swatch:** 4¹/₂" (11.5 cm) square
With Blue, ch 10.
Work same as Afghan Body for 8 rows.
Finish off.

## AFGHAN
With Blue, ch 96.

**Row 1:** Sc in second ch from hook and in each ch across: 95 sc.

**Row 2 (Right side):** Ch 1, turn; sc in first sc, (dc in next sc, sc in next sc) across.

**Note:** Loop a short piece of yarn around any stitch to mark Row 2 as **right** side.

**Row 3:** Ch 3 **(counts as first dc, now and throughout)**, turn; (sc in next dc, dc in next sc) across.

**Row 4:** Ch 1, turn; sc in first dc, (dc in next sc, sc in next dc) across.

**Row 5:** Ch 3, turn; (sc in next dc, dc in next sc) across.

**Rows 6-28:** Repeat Rows 4 and 5, 11 times; then repeat Row 4 once **more**.

Finish off.

**Row 29:** With **wrong** side facing, join Variegated with dc in first sc **(see Joining With Dc, page 122)**; (sc in next dc, dc in next sc) across.

**Rows 30-42:** Repeat Rows 4 and 5, 6 times; then repeat Row 4 once **more**.

Finish off.

**Row 43:** With **wrong** side facing, join Blue with dc in first sc; (sc in next dc, dc in next sc) across.

**Rows 44-70:** Repeat Rows 4 and 5, 13 times; then repeat Row 4 once **more**.

Finish off.

**Rows 71-111:** Repeat Rows 29-69; at end of Row 111, do **not** finish off.

**Row 112:** Ch 1, turn; sc in each st across; finish off.

*Design by Beverly Mewhorter.*

# OUTSTANDING

**MATERIALS**
Medium Weight Yarn 〔4〕
[3.5 ounces, 208 yards (100 grams, 190 meters) per skein]:
19 skeins
Crochet hook, size J (6 mm) **or** size needed for gauge

◼◼◼◻ **INTERMEDIATE**

**Finished Size:** 56$^{1}/_{2}$" x 74"
(143.5 cm x 188 cm)

**GAUGE:** In pattern, 8 rows = 4$^{1}/_{2}$" (11.5 cm)

**Gauge Swatch:** 7"w x 4$^{1}/_{2}$"h (17.75 cm x 11.5 cm)
Ch 25.
**Row 1:** Dc in fourth ch from hook **(3 skipped chs count as first dc)** and in next 6 chs, skip next 3 chs, 2 dc in next ch, (ch 1, 2 dc in same st) twice, skip next 3 chs, dc in last 8 chs: 22 dc and 2 ch-1 sps.
**Row 2** (Right side): Ch 3 **(counts as first dc, now and throughout)**, turn; skip next st, work FPdc around each of next 3 sts, work FPtr around skipped st, dc in next dc, work Popcorn in next dc, dc in next dc, work 2 FPtr around next dc, skip next 2 dc, 5 sc in sp **before** next dc **(Fig. 8, page 124)**, skip next 2 dc, work 2 FPtr around next dc, dc in next dc, work Popcorn in next dc, dc in next dc, skip next st, work FPdc around each of next 3 sts, work FPtr around skipped st, dc in last dc: 25 sts.

**Row 3:** Ch 3, turn; work BPdc around each of next 4 sts, dc in next 3 sts, skip next 4 sts, work Shell in next sc, skip next 4 sts, dc in next 3 sts, work BPdc around each of next 4 sts, dc in last dc: 22 sts and 2 ch-1 sps.
**Rows 4-8:** Repeat Rows 2 and 3 twice, then repeat Row 2 once **more**.
Finish off.

*Instructions continued on page 60.*

## STITCH GUIDE

### SHELL
2 Dc in st indicated, (ch 1, 2 dc in same st) twice.

### BACK POST DOUBLE CROCHET
#### (abbreviated BPdc)
YO, insert hook from **back** to **front** around post of st indicated *(Fig. 5, page 124)*, YO and pull up a loop even with loop on hook (3 loops on hook), (YO and draw through 2 loops on hook) twice.

### FRONT POST DOUBLE CROCHET
#### (abbreviated FPdc)
YO, insert hook from **front** to **back** around post of st indicated *(Fig. 5, page 124)*, YO and pull up a loop even with loop on hook (3 loops on hook), (YO and draw through 2 loops on hook) twice.

### FRONT POST TREBLE CROCHET *(abbreviated FPtr)*
YO twice, insert hook from **front** to **back** around post of st indicated *(Fig. 5, page 124)*, YO and pull up a loop (4 loops on hook), (YO and draw through 2 loops on hook) 3 times.

### POPCORN (uses one dc)
Work 4 dc in dc indicated, drop loop from hook, insert hook in first dc of 4-dc group, hook dropped loop and draw through st *(Fig. 6, page 124)*, ch 1 to close.

### PICOT
Ch 3, sc in third ch from hook.

## AFGHAN BODY
Ch 160; place marker in third ch from hook for Edging placement.

**Row 1** (Wrong side)**:** Dc in fourth ch from hook **(3 skipped chs count as first dc)** and in next 6 chs, † skip next 3 chs, work Shell in next ch, skip next 3 chs, dc in next 7 chs, skip next 3 chs, work Shell in next ch, skip next 3 chs, dc in next 3 chs, skip next 3 chs, work Shell in next ch, skip next 3 chs, dc in next 4 chs, skip next 3 chs, work Shell in next ch, skip next 3 chs, dc in next 3 chs, skip next 3 chs, work Shell in next ch, skip next 3 chs, dc in next 7 chs, skip next 3 chs, work Shell in next ch, skip next 3 chs †, dc in next 10 chs, repeat from † to † once, dc in last 8 chs: 146 dc and 24 ch-1 sps.

**Row 2:** Ch 3 **(counts as first dc, now and throughout)**, turn; skip next st, work FPdc around each of next 3 sts, work FPtr around skipped st, † dc in next dc, work Popcorn in next dc, dc in next dc, work 2 FPtr around next dc, skip next 2 dc, 5 sc in sp **before** next dc *(Fig. 8, page 124)*, skip next 2 dc, work 2 FPtr around next dc, dc in next dc, work Popcorn in next dc, dc in next dc, skip next st, work FPdc around each of next 3 sts, work FPtr around skipped st †, ♥ work 2 FPtr around next dc, skip next 2 dc, 5 sc in sp **before** next dc, skip next 2 dc, work 2 FPtr around next dc, dc in next dc, work Popcorn in next dc, dc in next dc, work 2 FPtr around next dc, skip next 2 dc, 5 sc in sp **before** next dc, skip next 2 dc, work 2 FPtr around next dc, skip next st, work FPdc around each of next 3 sts, work FPtr around skipped st ♥; repeat from ♥ to ♥ once **more**, then repeat from † to † twice, repeat from ♥ to ♥ twice, then repeat from † to † once, dc in last dc: 182 sts.

**Row 3:** Ch 3, turn; † work BPdc around each of next 4 sts, dc in next 3 sts, skip next 4 sts, work Shell in next sc, skip next 4 sts, dc in next 3 sts †, ♥ work BPdc around each of next 4 sts, skip next 4 sts, work Shell in next sc, skip next 4 sts, dc in next 3 sts, skip next 4 sts, work Shell in next sc, skip next 4 sts ♥; repeat from ♥ to ♥ once **more**, then repeat from † to † twice, repeat from ♥ to ♥ twice, then repeat from † to † once, work BPdc around each of next 4 sts, dc in last dc: 146 sts and 24 ch-1 sps.

**Rows 4-125:** Repeat Rows 2 and 3, 61 times.

**Row 126:** Ch 3, turn; skip next st, work FPdc around each of next 3 sts, work FPtr around skipped st, † dc in next dc, work Popcorn in next dc, dc in next dc, work 2 FPtr around next dc, skip next 2 dc, 3 sc in sp **before** next dc, skip next 2 dc, work 2 FPtr around next dc, dc in next dc, work Popcorn in next dc, dc in next dc, skip next st, work FPdc around each of next 3 sts, work FPtr around skipped st †, ♥ work 2 FPtr around next dc, skip next 2 dc, 3 sc in sp **before** next dc, skip next 2 dc, work 2 FPtr around next dc, dc in next dc, work Popcorn in next dc, dc in next dc, work 2 FPtr around next dc, skip next 2 dc, 3 sc in sp **before** next dc, skip next 2 dc, work 2 FPtr around next dc, skip next st, work FPdc around each of next 3 sts, work FPtr around skipped st ♥; repeat from ♥ to ♥ once **more**, then repeat from † to † twice, repeat from ♥ to ♥ twice, then repeat from † to † once, dc in last dc; do **not** finish off: 158 sts.

## EDGING

**Rnd 1:** Ch 3, do **not** turn; dc in last dc made on Row 126, skip first row, working around dc at end of rows, dc around next row, † skip next row, work Shell around next row, skip next row, dc around next row †; repeat from † to † across; working in free loops of beginning ch *(Fig. 4b, page 123)*, work Shell in marked ch, skip next 3 chs, dc in next ch, skip next 2 chs, work Shell in next ch, (skip next 2 chs, dc in next ch, skip next 2 chs, work Shell in next ch) across; skip first row, working around dc at end of rows, dc around next row, repeat from † to † across; working across Row 126, work Shell in first dc, skip next 2 sts, dc in next st, (skip next 2 sts, work Shell in next st, skip next 2 sts, dc in next st) across to last 3 sts, skip last 3 sts, (2 dc in same dc as first dc made, ch 1) twice; join with slip st to first dc.

**Rnd 2:** Turn; slip st in first ch-1 sp, ch 1, (sc, work Picot, sc) in same sp, ch 4, (sc, work Picot, sc) in next ch-1 sp, ch 4, skip next 2 dc, work FPdc around next dc, ch 4, ★ † skip next 3 dc, (sc, work Picot, sc) in sp **before** next dc, ch 4, skip next 3 dc, work FPdc around next dc, ch 4 †; repeat from † to † across to next corner 6-dc group, [(sc, work Picot, sc) in next ch-1 sp, ch 4] twice, skip next 2 dc, work FPdc around next dc, ch 4; repeat from ★ 2 times **more**, then repeat from † to † across; join with slip st to first sc, finish off.

*Design by Barbara Shaffer.*

# HILL & VALLEY

## MATERIALS

Medium Weight Yarn 🧶4

[3.5 ounces, 170 yards (100 grams, 156 meters) per skein]:
  Brown - 12 skeins
  Green - 5 skeins
Crochet hook, size J (6 mm) **or** size needed for gauge

■■■▢▢ **INTERMEDIATE**

**Finished Size:** 47" x 65"
(119.5 cm x 165 cm)

**GAUGE:** One repeat (from point to point) =
  $5^3/_4$" (14.5 cm); 8 rows = $4^1/_2$" (11.5 cm)

**Gauge Swatch:** $11^1/_2$" x $4^1/_2$"
  (29.25 cm x 11.5 cm)
With Brown, ch 44.
Work same as Body Rows 1-8.
Finish off.

## STITCH GUIDE

**POPCORN** (uses one dc)
4 Dc in dc indicated, drop loop from hook, insert
hook in first dc of 4-dc group, hook dropped loop
and draw through st **(Fig. 6, page 124)**, ch 1 to
close.

**FRONT POST DOUBLE CROCHET (abbreviated FPdc)**
YO, insert hook from **front** to **back** around post of
st indicated **(Fig. 5, page 124)**, YO and pull up
a loop (3 loops on hook), (YO and draw through
2 loops on hook) twice.

**BACK POST DOUBLE CROCHET (abbreviated BPdc)**
YO, insert hook from **back** to **front** around post of
dc indicated **(Fig. 5, page 124)**, YO and pull up
a loop (3 loops on hook), (YO and draw through
2 loops on hook) twice.

## BODY

With Brown, ch 170; place marker in third ch
from hook for st placement.

**Row 1:** Dc in fifth ch from hook **(4 skipped chs
count as first dc and one skipped ch)**, ch 1, dc in
same st, [skip next 2 chs, (dc, ch 1, dc) in next
ch] twice, skip next ch, 3 dc in next ch, skip next
ch, (dc, ch 1, dc) in next ch, [skip next 2 chs,
(dc, ch 1, dc) in next ch] twice, ★ skip next
4 chs, (dc, ch 1, dc) in next ch, [skip next 2 chs,
(dc, ch 1, dc) in next ch] twice, skip next ch, 3 dc
in next ch, skip next ch, (dc, ch 1, dc) in next ch,
[skip next 2 chs, (dc, ch 1, dc) in next ch] twice;
repeat from ★ across to last 2 chs, skip next ch,
dc in last ch: 122 dc and 48 ch-1 sps.

*Instructions continued on page 64.*

**Row 2** (Right side)**:** Ch 3 **(counts as first dc, now and throughout)**, turn; (skip next dc, work Popcorn in next dc, ch 2) 3 times, work FPdc around next dc, dc in next dc, work FPdc around next dc, ch 2, work Popcorn in next dc, (ch 2, skip next dc, work Popcorn in next dc) twice, ★ skip next 2 dc, work Popcorn in next dc, ch 2, (skip next dc, work Popcorn in next dc, ch 2) twice, work FPdc around next dc, dc in next dc, work FPdc around next dc, ch 2, work Popcorn in next dc, (ch 2, skip next dc, work Popcorn in next dc) twice; repeat from ★ across to last 2 dc, skip next dc, dc in last dc: 74 sts and 48 ch-2 sps.

**Row 3:** Ch 3, turn; 3 dc in each of next 3 ch-2 sps, skip next FPdc, 3 dc in next dc, ★ 3 dc in each of next 6 ch-2 sps, skip next FPdc, 3 dc in next dc; repeat from ★ across to last 3 ch-2 sps, 3 dc in each of last 3 ch-2 sps, skip last Popcorn, dc in last dc changing to Green **(Fig. 3b, page 123)**: 170 dc.

**Row 4:** Ch 3, turn; skip next dc, (work BPdc around each of next 2 dc, work FPdc around next dc) 3 times, 3 dc in next dc, (work FPdc around next dc, work BPdc around each of next 2 dc) 3 times, ★ skip next 2 dc, (work BPdc around each of next 2 dc, work FPdc around next dc) 3 times, 3 dc in next dc, (work FPdc around next dc, work BPdc around each of next 2 dc) 3 times; repeat from ★ across to last 2 dc, skip next dc, dc in last dc.

**Row 5:** Ch 2 **(counts as first hdc)**, turn; skip next BPdc, hdc in next 9 sts, 3 hdc in next dc, hdc in next 9 sts, ★ skip next 2 BPdc, hdc in next 9 sts, 3 hdc in next dc, hdc in next 9 sts; repeat from ★ across to last 2 sts, skip next BPdc, hdc in last dc.

**Row 6:** Ch 1, turn; working in Back Loops Only **(Fig. 2, page 123)**, sc in first hdc, skip next hdc, (work FPdc around FPdc one row **below** next hdc, skip next hdc, sc in next 2 hdc) 3 times, 3 sc in next hdc, sc in next 2 hdc, work FPdc around FPdc one row **below** next hdc, (skip next hdc, sc in next 2 hdc, work FPdc around FPdc one row **below** next hdc) twice, ★ skip next 3 hdc, (work FPdc around FPdc one row **below** next hdc, skip next hdc, sc in next 2 hdc) 3 times, 3 sc in next hdc, sc in next 2 hdc, work FPdc around FPdc one row **below** next hdc, (skip next hdc, sc in next 2 hdc, work FPdc around FPdc one row **below** next hdc) twice; repeat from ★ across to last 3 hdc, skip next 2 hdc, sc in last hdc changing to Brown **(Fig. 3a, page 123)**.

**Row 7:** Ch 3, turn; skip next FPdc, working in both loops, dc in next 9 sts, 3 dc in next sc, dc in next 9 sts, ★ skip next 2 FPdc, dc in next 9 sts, 3 dc in next sc, dc in next 9 sts; repeat from ★ across to last 2 sts, skip next FPdc, dc in last sc.

**Row 8:** Ch 3, turn; skip next dc, work FPdc around next dc, work BPdc around each of next 7 dc, work FPdc around next dc, 3 dc in next dc, work FPdc around next dc, work BPdc around each of next 7 dc, work FPdc around next dc, ★ skip next 2 dc, work FPdc around next dc, work BPdc around each of next 7 dc, work FPdc around next dc, 3 dc in next dc, work FPdc around next dc, work BPdc around each of next 7 dc, work FPdc around next dc; repeat from ★ across to last 2 dc, skip next dc, dc in last dc.

**Row 9:** Ch 3, turn; [skip next 2 sts, (dc, ch 1, dc) in next st] 3 times, skip next dc, 3 dc in next dc, skip next dc, (dc, ch 1, dc) in next FPdc, [skip next 2 sts, (dc, ch 1, dc) in next st] twice, ★ skip next 4 sts, (dc, ch 1, dc) in next BPdc, [skip next 2 sts, (dc, ch 1, dc) in next st] twice, skip next dc, 3 dc in next dc, skip next dc, (dc, ch 1, dc) in next FPdc, [skip next 2 sts, (dc, ch 1, dc) in next st] twice; repeat from ★ across to last 3 sts, skip next 2 sts, dc in last dc: 122 dc and 48 ch-1 sps.

**Rows 10-114:** Repeat Rows 2-9, 13 times; then repeat Row 2 once **more**; at end of Row 114, do **not** finish off.

## EDGING

Ch 4 **(counts as first dc plus ch 1)**, do **not** turn; [dc, (ch 1, dc) twice] in top of last dc on Row 114; working in end of rows, skip first 2 rows, (dc, ch 1, dc) in each of next 2 rows, [skip next 2 rows, (dc, ch 1, dc) in each of next 6 rows] across to last 6 rows, skip next 2 rows, (dc, ch 1, dc) in each of next 3 rows, skip last row; working in free loops of beginning ch *(Fig. 4b, page 123)*, [dc, (ch 1, dc) 3 times] in marked ch, skip next ch, (dc, ch 1, dc) in next ch, [skip next 2 chs, (dc, ch 1, dc) in next ch] twice, skip next 3 chs, (dc, ch 1, dc) in next ch, [skip next 2 chs, (dc, ch 1, dc) in next ch] twice, ★ [dc, (ch 1, dc) 3 times] in next sp, (dc, ch 1, dc) in next ch, [skip next 2 chs, (dc, ch 1, dc) in next ch] twice, skip next 3 chs, (dc, ch 1, dc) in next ch, [skip next 2 chs, (dc, ch 1, dc) in next ch] twice; repeat from ★ across to last 2 chs, skip next ch, [dc, (ch 1, dc) 3 times] in last ch; working in end of rows, skip first row, (dc, ch 1, dc) in each of next 3 rows, [skip next 2 rows, (dc, ch 1, dc) in each of next 6 rows] across to last 6 rows, skip next 2 rows, (dc, ch 1, dc) in each of next 2 rows, skip last 2 rows; working in sts and sps across Row 114, [dc, (ch 1, dc) 3 times] in first dc, (dc, ch 1, dc) in each of next 3 ch-2 sps, skip next FPdc, [dc, (ch 1, dc) 3 times] in next dc, † (dc, ch 1, dc) in each of next 6 ch-2 sps, skip next FPdc, [dc, (ch 1, dc) 3 times] in next dc †; repeat from † to † across to last 3 ch-2 sps, (dc, ch 1, dc) in each of last 3 ch-2 sps; join with slip st to first dc, finish off.

*Design by Barbara Shaffer.*

# TRANQUILITY

**MATERIALS**

Medium Weight Yarn **4** MEDIUM

[3.5 ounces, 170 yards (100 grams, 156 meters) per skein]:
17 skeins
Crochet hook, size J (6 mm) **or** size needed for gauge

■■■◻ INTERMEDIATE

**Finished Size:** 48¹/₂" x 66"
(123 cm x 167.5 cm)

**GAUGE:** In pattern,
  12 sts and 7 rows = 4" (10 cm)

**Gauge Swatch:** 4¹/₄"w x 4"h (10.75 cm x 10 cm)
Ch 15.
Work same as Body Rows 1-7.
Finish off.

## STITCH GUIDE

### BACK POST DOUBLE CROCHET
  *(abbreviated BPdc)*
YO, insert hook from **back** to **front** around post
of dc indicated *(Fig. 5, page 124)*, YO and pull
up a loop (3 loops on hook), (YO and draw
through 2 loops on hook) twice.

### FRONT POST TREBLE CROCHET *(abbreviated FPtr)*
YO twice, insert hook from **front** to **back**
around post of dc indicated *(Fig. 5, page 124)*,
YO and pull up a loop (4 loops on hook), (YO
and draw through 2 loops on hook) 3 times.

### BEGINNING POPCORN (uses one ch-1 sp)
Ch 3 **(counts as first dc)**, 3 dc in sp indicated,
drop loop from hook, insert hook in first dc
of 4-dc group, hook dropped loop and draw
through st, ch 1 to close.

### POPCORN (uses one sp)
4 Dc in sp indicated, drop loop from hook,
insert hook in first dc of 4-dc group, hook
dropped loop and draw through st *(Fig. 6,
page 124)*, ch 1 to close.

## BODY

Ch 135; place marker in third ch from hook for st
placement.

**Row 1:** Dc in fourth ch from hook **(3 skipped chs
count as first dc)** and in each ch across: 133 dc.

**Row 2** (Right side)**:** Ch 3 **(counts as first dc, now
and throughout)**, turn; work BPdc around next dc,
work FPtr around next dc, ★ work BPdc around
each of next 3 dc, work FPtr around next dc;
repeat from ★ across to last 2 dc, work BPdc
around next dc, dc in last dc.

**Row 3:** Ch 3, turn; skip next BPdc, 4 dc in next
FPtr, (skip next 3 BPdc, 4 dc in next FPtr) across
to last 2 sts, skip next BPdc, dc in last dc:
134 dc.

**Row 4:** Ch 5 **(counts as first dc plus ch 2, now and
throughout)**, turn; skip next 2 dc, work Popcorn in
sp **before** next dc *(Fig. 8, page 124)*, ★ ch 1, skip
next 2 dc, dc in sp **before** next dc, ch 2, skip next
2 dc, work Popcorn in sp **before** next dc; repeat
from ★ across to last 3 dc, ch 2, skip next 2 dc,
dc in last dc: 67 sts and 66 sps.

*Instructions continued on page 71.*

# AUTUMN

**MATERIALS**
Medium Weight Yarn **(4)** MEDIUM
[3.5 ounces, 205 yards (100 grams, 187 meters) per skein]:
  Ecru - 8 skeins
  Brown - 4 skeins
  Green and Gold - 3 skeins **each** color
Crochet hook, size I (5.5 mm) **or** size needed for gauge
Yarn needle

◼◼◻◻ **EASY**

**Finished Size:** 46" x 68"
(117 cm x 172.5 cm)

**GAUGE:** Rnds 1-3 = 4" (10 cm)
        Each Square = 5½" (14 cm)

## STITCH GUIDE
**TREBLE CROCHET (abbreviated tr)**
YO twice, insert hook in st indicated, YO and pull up a loop (4 loops on hook), (YO and draw through 2 loops on hook) 3 times.
**DOUBLE TREBLE CROCHET (abbreviated dtr)**
YO 3 times, insert hook in st indicated, YO and pull up a loop (5 loops on hook), (YO and draw through 2 loops on hook) 4 times.

## SQUARE (Make 96 total)
Make 32 Squares **each** using the following colors for Rnds 4 and 5: Green, Gold, and Brown.

With Ecru, ch 4; join with slip st to form a ring.

**Rnd 1** (Right side)**:** Ch 3 **(counts as first dc, now and throughout)**, 2 dc in ring, ch 3, (3 dc in ring, ch 3) 3 times; join with slip st to BLO of first dc **(Fig. 2, page 123)**: 12 dc and 4 ch-3 sps.

**Note:** Loop a short piece of yarn around any stitch to mark Rnd 1 as **right** side.

**Rnds 2 and 3:** Ch 3, ★ dc in BLO of next dc and each dc across to next ch-3 sp, (2 dc, ch 3, 2 dc) in ch-3 sp; repeat from ★ 3 times **more**, dc in BLO of next dc and each dc across; join with slip st to BLO of first dc: 44 dc and 4 ch-3 sps.

Finish off.

**Rnd 4:** With **right** side facing, join color indicated with slip st in any corner ch-3 sp; ch 3, dc in same sp, ★ † dc in both loops of next 3 dc, tr in free loop of dc one rnd **below** next dc (on Rnd 2) **(Fig. 4a, page 123)**, skip st behind tr, dc in both loops next dc (on Rnd 3), dtr in free loop of dc two rnds **below** next dc (on Rnd 1), skip st behind dtr, dc in both loops of next dc (on Rnd 3), tr in free loop of dc one rnd **below** next dc (on Rnd 2), skip st behind tr, dc in both loops of next 3 dc (on Rnd 3) †, (2 dc, ch 3, 2 dc) in next corner ch-3 sp; repeat from ★ 2 times **more**, then repeat from † to † once, 2 dc in same corner as first dc, ch 1, hdc in first dc to form last ch-3 sp: 60 sts and 4 ch-3 sps.

*Instructions continued on page 70.*

continued from AUTUMN page 68

**Rnd 5:** Ch 1, 2 sc in last ch-3 sp made, ★ sc in each st across to next corner ch-3 sp, 3 sc in corner ch-3 sp; repeat from ★ 2 times **more**, sc in each st across and in same sp as first sc; join with slip st to first sc, finish off leaving a long end for sewing: 72 sc.

## ASSEMBLY

With long end and using Placement Diagram as a guide, whipstitch Squares together forming 8 vertical strips of 12 Squares each **(Fig. 9b, page 125)**, working through **inside** loops on **both** pieces, and beginning in center sc of first corner and ending in center sc of next corner; then whipstitch strips together in same manner.

## EDGING

**Rnd 1:** With **right** side of short edge facing, join Brown with slip st in center sc of first corner 3-sc group; ch 1, 2 sc in same st, † work 137 sc evenly spaced across to center sc of next corner 3-sc group, 3 sc in center sc, work 205 sc evenly spaced across to center sc of next corner 3-sc group †, 3 sc in center sc, repeat from † to † once, sc in same st as first sc; join with slip st to first sc: 696 sc.

**Rnd 2:** Ch 1, (sc, ch 4) twice in same st as joining, skip next sc, ★ (sc in next sc, ch 4, skip next sc) across to center sc of next corner 3-sc group, (sc, ch 4) twice in center sc, skip next sc; repeat from ★ 2 times **more**, (sc in next sc, ch 4, skip next sc) across; join with slip st to first sc, finish off.

*Design by Maggie Weldon.*

#### PLACEMENT DIAGRAM

| C | B | A | C | B | A | C | B |
|---|---|---|---|---|---|---|---|
| B | A | C | B | A | C | B | A |
| A | C | B | A | C | B | A | C |
| C | B | A | C | B | A | C | B |
| B | A | C | B | A | C | B | A |
| A | C | B | A | C | B | A | C |
| C | B | A | C | B | A | C | B |
| B | A | C | B | A | C | B | A |
| A | C | B | A | C | B | A | C |
| C | B | A | C | B | A | C | B |
| B | A | C | B | A | C | B | A |
| A | C | B | A | C | B | A | C |

**KEY**

**A - Green**      **B - Gold**      **C - Brown**

**Row 5:** Ch 3, turn; dc in next sp and in each st and each sp across: 133 dc.

**Row 6:** Ch 3, turn; work BPdc around next dc, work FPtr around next dc, ★ work BPdc around each of next 3 dc, work FPtr around next dc; repeat from ★ across to last 2 dc, work BPdc around next dc, dc in last dc.

**Row 7:** Ch 3, turn; dc in next st and in each st across.

**Row 8:** Ch 3, turn; work BPdc around next dc, work FPtr around next dc, ★ work BPdc around each of next 3 dc, work FPtr around next dc; repeat from ★ across to last 2 dc, work BPdc around next dc, dc in last dc.

**Row 9:** Ch 3, turn; skip next BPdc, 4 dc in next FPtr, (skip next 3 BPdc, 4 dc in next FPtr) across to last 2 sts, skip next BPdc, dc in last dc: 134 dc.

**Row 10:** Ch 5, turn; skip next 2 dc, work Popcorn in sp **before** next dc, ★ ch 1, skip next 2 dc, dc in sp **before** next dc, ch 2, skip next 2 dc, work Popcorn in sp **before** next dc; repeat from ★ across to last 3 dc, ch 2, skip next 2 dc, dc in last dc: 67 sts and 66 sps.

**Rows 11-108:** Repeat Rows 5-10, 16 times; then repeat Rows 5 and 6 once **more**; do **not** finish off.

## EDGING

**Rnd 1** (Right side)**:** Ch 4 **(counts as first dc plus ch 1)**, do **not** turn; [dc, (ch 1, dc) twice] in top of last dc on Row 108; working in end of rows, skip first row, (dc, ch 1, dc) in next row, [skip next row, (dc, ch 1, dc) in next row] across to last 4 rows, skip next row, (dc, ch 1, dc) in each of next 2 rows, skip last row; working in free loops of beginning ch **(Fig. 4b, page 123)**, [dc, (ch 1, dc) twice] in marked ch, [skip next 3 chs, (dc, ch 1, dc) in next ch] across to last 4 chs, skip next 3 chs, [dc, (ch 1, dc) twice] in last ch; working in end of rows, skip first row, (dc, ch 1, dc) in each of next 2 rows, skip next row, [(dc, ch 1, dc) in next row, skip next row] across; working in sts across Row 108, [dc, (ch 1, dc) twice] in first dc, skip next 3 sts, [(dc, ch 1, dc) in next st, skip next 3 sts] across; join with slip st to first dc: 108 ch-1 sps.

**Rnd 2:** Turn; slip st in first ch-1 sp, ch 3, (dc, ch 1, 2 dc) in same sp, (2 dc, ch 1, 2 dc) in next ch-1 sp and in each ch-1 sp around; join with slip st to first dc.

**Rnd 3:** Turn; slip st in next 2 dc and in next ch-1 sp, work Beginning Popcorn in same sp, ch 5, (work Popcorn in next ch-1 sp, ch 5) around; join with slip st to top of Beginning Popcorn, finish off.

*Design by Barbara Shaffer.*

# TEMPTING TAUPE

**MATERIALS**
Medium Weight Yarn **[MEDIUM 4]**
[3.5 ounces, 170 yards (100 grams, 156 meters) per skein]:
  20 skeins
Crochet hook, size I (5.5 mm) **or** size needed for gauge

**☐☐☐☐☐ EASY**

**Finished Size:** 56" x 71¹/₂"
(142 cm x 181.5 cm)

**GAUGE:** In pattern,
  17 sts and 8 rows = 5" (12.75 cm)
  Each Panel = 7¹/₂" (19 cm) wide

## STITCH GUIDE

### BACK POST DOUBLE CROCHET
#### (abbreviated BPdc)
YO, insert hook from **back** to **front** around post of st indicated (**Fig. 5, page 124**), YO and pull up a loop (3 loops on hook), (YO and draw through 2 loops on hook) twice.

### FRONT POST DOUBLE CROCHET
#### (abbreviated FPdc)
YO, insert hook from **front** to **back** around post of st indicated (**Fig. 5, page 124**), YO and pull up a loop (3 loops on hook), (YO and draw through 2 loops on hook) twice.

## PANEL (Make 7)
Ch 19.

**Row 1** (Right side): (Dc, ch 3, dc) in sixth ch from hook **(5 skipped chs count as first dc and 2 skipped chs)**, ★ skip next 4 chs, (dc, ch 3, dc) in next ch; repeat from ★ once **more**, skip next 2 chs, dc in last ch: 8 dc and 3 ch-3 sps.

**Note:** Loop a short piece of yarn around any stitch to mark Row 1 as **right** side and **bottom** edge.

**Row 2:** Ch 3 **(counts as first dc, now and throughout)**, turn; 5 dc in each of next 3 ch-3 sps, skip next dc, dc in last dc: 17 dc.

**Row 3:** Ch 3, turn; dc in BLO of next dc and each dc across **(Fig. 2, page 123)**.

**Row 4:** Ch 3, turn; work BPdc around next dc, (work FPdc around next dc, work BPdc around next dc) across to last dc, dc in last dc.

**Row 5:** Ch 3, turn; working in both loops, skip next 2 sts, (dc, ch 3, dc) in next st, ★ skip next 4 sts, (dc, ch 3, dc) in next st; repeat from ★ once **more**, skip next 2 sts, dc in last dc: 8 dc and 3 ch-3 sps.

**Rows 6-105:** Repeat Rows 2-5, 25 times; do **not** finish off.

*Instructions continued on page 77.*

# INCREDIBLE IN WHITE

## MATERIALS

Medium Weight Yarn (4)
[6 ounces, 312 yards (170 grams, 285 meters) per skein]:
   9 skeins
Crochet hook, size I (5.5 mm) **or** size needed for gauge
Yarn needle

**EASY +**

**Finished Size:** 50" x 67"
(127 cm x 170 cm)

**GAUGE:** Each Square = 5³/₄" (14.5 cm)

**Gauge Swatch:** 2³/₄" (7 cm) square
Work same as Square through Rnd 2.

## STITCH GUIDE

### TREBLE CROCHET *(abbreviated tr)*

YO twice, insert hook in st indicated, YO and
pull up a loop (4 loops on hook), (YO and
draw through 2 loops on hook) 3 times.

### CROSS ST

Tr in next st, ch 1, working in **front** of last
tr made, tr in same st as first tr of previous
Cross St made.

## SQUARE (Make 88)

**Rnd 1** (Right side)**:** Ch 2, 8 sc in second ch from
hook; join with slip st to first sc.

**Note:** Loop a short piece of yarn around any stitch
to mark Rnd 1 as **right** side.

**Rnd 2:** Ch 5 **(counts as first tr plus ch 1, now and
throughout)**, working in **front** of tr just made, tr
in last sc on Rnd 1 **(first Cross St made)**, work
6 Cross Sts, tr in same st as second tr of first
Cross St made, ch 1, working in **front** of last tr
made, tr in same st as first tr made of previous
Cross St; join with slip st to first tr: 8 Cross Sts.

**Rnd 3:** Slip st in next ch and in next tr, ch 5,
working in **front** of tr just made, tr in same st
as joining, work 14 Cross Sts, tr in same st as
second tr of first Cross St made, ch 1, working
in **front** of last tr made, tr in same st as first tr of
previous Cross St made; join with slip st to first tr:
16 Cross Sts.

**Rnd 4:** (Slip st, ch 1, sc) in first ch-1 sp, ch 6,
tr in sixth ch from hook, ch 1, sc in next ch-1 sp,
★ (ch 4, sc in next ch-1 sp) 3 times, ch 6, tr in
sixth ch from hook, ch 1, sc in next ch-1 sp;
repeat from ★ 2 times **more**, (ch 4, sc in next
ch-1 sp) twice, ch 1, dc in first sc to form last
ch-4 sp: 16 sps.

*Instructions continued on page 76.*

**Rnd 5:** Ch 4 **(counts as first hdc plus ch 2)**, (3 dc, ch 3, 3 dc) in next corner sp, ch 2, hdc in next ch-4 sp, ch 2, sc in next ch-4 sp, ch 2, ★ hdc in next ch-4 sp, ch 2, (3 dc, ch 3, 3 dc) in next corner sp, ch 2, hdc in next ch-4 sp, ch 2, sc in next ch-4 sp, ch 2; repeat from ★ 2 times **more**; join with slip st to first hdc, finish off: 36 sts and 20 sps.

## ASSEMBLY

Working through **both** loops on **both** pieces, whipstitch Squares together **(Fig. 9a, page 125)**, forming 8 vertical strips of 11 Squares each, beginning in center ch of first corner ch-3 and ending in center ch of next corner ch-3; then whipstitch strips together in same manner.

## EDGING

**Rnd 1:** With **right** side facing, join yarn with sc in any corner ch-3 sp **(see Joining With Sc, page 122)**; ch 3, sc in same sp, ★ † ch 1, skip next dc, sc in next dc, ch 1, sc in next ch-2 sp, ch 1, sc in next hdc, ch 1, (sc in next ch-2 sp, ch 1) twice, sc in next hdc, ch 1, sc in next ch-2 sp, ch 1, skip next dc, sc in next dc, ch 1, [(sc in next sp, ch 1) twice, skip next dc, sc in next dc, ch 1, sc in next ch-2 sp, ch 1, sc in next hdc, ch 1, (sc in next ch-2 sp, ch 1) twice, sc in next hdc, ch 1, sc in next ch-2 sp, ch 1, skip next dc, sc in next dc, ch 1] across to next corner ch-3 sp †, (sc, ch 3, sc) in corner ch-3 sp; repeat from ★ 2 times **more**, then repeat from † to † once; join with slip st to first sc: 380 sps.

**Rnd 2:** Slip st in next corner ch-3 sp, ch 1, ★ (sc, ch 3, sc) in corner ch-3 sp, ch 1, (sc in next ch-1 sp, ch 1) across to next corner ch-3 sp; repeat from ★ around; join with slip st to first sc: 384 sps.

**Rnd 3:** Ch 4 **(counts as first dc plus ch 1, now and throughout)**, ★ † (dc, ch 1) 4 times in corner ch-3 sp **(Corner Shell made)**, skip next ch-1 sp, (sc in next ch-1 sp, ch 1) 3 times, [skip next sc, (dc, ch 1) 3 times in next sc, skip next ch-1 sp, (sc in next ch-1 sp, ch 1) 3 times] across to within 2 sc of next corner ch-3 sp, skip next sc †, dc in next sc, ch 1; repeat from ★ 2 times **more**, then repeat from † to † once; join with slip st to first dc: 236 dc and 464 ch-1 sps.

**Rnd 4:** Ch 4, ★ † (dc in next ch-1 sp, ch 1, dc in next dc, ch 1) 4 times, skip next ch-1 sp, (sc in next ch-1 sp, ch 1) twice, [skip next sc, dc in next dc, ch 1, (dc in next ch-1 sp, ch 1, dc in next dc, ch 1) twice, skip next ch-1 sp, (sc in next ch-1 sp, ch 1) twice] across to within one sc of next Corner Shell, skip next sc †, dc in next dc, ch 1; repeat from ★ 2 times **more**, then repeat from † to † once; join with slip st to first dc.

**Rnd 5:** ★ † (Ch 2, slip st in next dc) 8 times, ch 1, skip next ch-1 sp, slip st in next ch-1 sp, ch 1, [skip next sc, slip st in next dc, (ch 2, slip st in next dc) 4 times, ch 1, skip next ch-1 sp, slip st in next ch-1 sp, ch 1] across to within one sc of next Corner Shell, skip next sc †, slip st in next dc; repeat from ★ 2 times **more**, then repeat from † to † once; join with slip st to joining slip st, finish off.

*Design by Anne Halliday.*

## BORDER

**Rnd 1:** Ch 3, do **not** turn; 4 dc in last dc made on Row 105 (corner); work 2 dc in end of each row across; working in free loops of beginning ch **(Fig. 4b, page 123)**, 5 dc in first ch (corner), dc in next 15 chs, 5 dc in next ch (corner); work 2 dc in end of each row across; working in sts on Row 105, 5 dc in first dc (corner), dc in each dc and in each ch across; join with slip st to first dc: 470 dc.

**Rnd 2:** Ch 1, work FPdc around same st as joining, work BPdc around next dc, (work FPdc around next dc, work BPdc around next dc) around; join with slip st to first FPdc.

**Rnd 3:** Ch 1, turn; hdc in same st as joining and in next 17 sts, 3 hdc in next st (corner), hdc in next 214 sts, 3 hdc in next st (corner), hdc in next 19 sts, 3 hdc in next st (corner), hdc in next 214 sts, 3 hdc in next st (corner), hdc in last st; join with slip st to first hdc: 478 hdc.

**Rnd 4:** Ch 1, turn; working in BLO, sc in same st as joining and in next 2 hdc, 3 sc in next corner hdc, ★ sc in next hdc and in each hdc across to center hdc of next corner 3-hdc group, 3 sc in corner hdc; repeat from ★ 2 times **more**, sc in next hdc and in each hdc across; join with slip st to **both** loops of first sc, finish off.

## ASSEMBLY

Join long edge of 2 Panels together as follows:

With **right** sides together, bottom edges to your right, and working through **both** thicknesses and in **outside** loops on **both** pieces, join yarn with sc in center sc of corner **(see Joining With Sc, page 122)**; sc in next sc and in each sc across through center sc of next corner; finish off.

Join remaining Panels in same manner.

## EDGING

**Rnd 1:** With **right** side of short edge facing, join yarn with dc in BLO of center sc of first corner 3-sc group **(see Joining With Dc, page 122)**; dc in same st as joining and in BLO of next 23 dc, † [dc in BLO of same st as joining on same Panel and in end of joining sc, dc in BLO of same st as joining on next Panel and in next 23 sc] across to center sc of next corner 3-sc group, 3 dc in BLO of corner sc, dc in BLO of next sc and each sc across to center sc of next corner 3-sc group †, 3 dc in BLO of corner sc, dc in BLO of next 23 dc, repeat from † to † once, dc in BLO of same st as joining; join with slip st to **both** loops of first dc: 806 dc.

**Rnd 2:** Ch 1, turn; working in both loops, 2 hdc in same st as joining, ★ hdc in next dc and in each dc across to center dc of next corner 3-dc group, 3 hdc in corner dc; repeat from ★ 2 times **more**, hdc in next dc and in each dc across, hdc in same st as joining; join with slip st to first hdc: 814 hdc.

**Rnd 3:** Ch 1, turn; (sc, ch 2, 2 dc) in same st as joining, skip next 3 hdc, ★ (sc, ch 2, 2 dc) in next hdc, skip next 2 hdc; repeat from ★ around; join with slip st to first sc, finish off.

*Design by Barbara Shaffer.*

# SWEET TANGERINE

**MATERIALS**
Medium Weight Yarn ( **4** )
[5 ounces, 256 yards (140 grams, 234 meters) per skein]:
  14 skeins
Crochet hook, size J (6 mm) **or** size needed for gauge

◼◼◼◻ **INTERMEDIATE**

**Finished Size:** 50" x 74"
(127 cm x 188 cm)

**GAUGE:** In pattern,
  2 repeats (34 sts) = $10^1/_2$" (26.75 cm);
  12 rows = $5^3/_4$" (14.5 cm)

**Gauge Swatch:** $7^1/_2$"w x $5^3/_4$"h (19 cm x 14.5 cm)
Ch 29.
**Row 1:** Dc in fourth ch from hook **(3 skipped chs count as first dc)** and in next 7 chs, skip next ch, 3 dc in next ch, (skip next 2 chs, 3 dc in next ch) twice, skip next ch, dc in last 9 chs: 27 dc.
**Rows 2-12:** Work same as Body.
Finish off.

## STITCH GUIDE

**FRONT POST DOUBLE CROCHET**
  **(abbreviated FPdc)**
YO, insert hook from **front** to **back** around post of st indicated **(Fig. 5, page 124)**, YO and pull up a loop (3 loops on hook), (YO and draw through 2 loops on hook) twice.

**BACK POST DOUBLE CROCHET**
  **(abbreviated BPdc)**
YO, insert hook from **back** to **front** around post of st indicated **(Fig. 5, page 124)**, YO and pull up a loop (3 loops on hook), (YO and draw through 2 loops on hook) twice.

**FRONT POST TREBLE CROCHET (abbreviated FPtr)**
YO twice, insert hook from **front** to **back** around post of st indicated **(Fig. 5, page 124)**, YO and pull up a loop (4 loops on hook), (YO and draw through 2 loops on hook) 3 times.

**CABLE** (uses next 4 sts)
Skip next st, work FPdc around each of next 3 sts, working in **front** of sts just made, work FPtr around skipped st.

**PICOT**
Ch 3, sc in third ch from hook.

## BODY

Ch 148; place marker in third ch from hook for Edging placement.

**Row 1:** Dc in fourth ch from hook **(3 skipped chs count as first dc)** and in next 7 chs, skip next ch, 3 dc in next ch, (skip next 2 chs, 3 dc in next ch) twice, ★ skip next ch, dc in next 8 chs, skip next ch, 3 dc in next ch, (skip next 2 chs, 3 dc in next ch) twice; repeat from ★ across to last 10 chs, skip next ch, dc in last 9 chs: 146 dc.

**Row 2 (Right side):** Ch 1, turn; sc in first dc, work Cable twice, ★ (work 2 FPtr around next dc, skip next dc, sc in next dc) 3 times, work Cable twice; repeat from ★ across to last dc, sc in last dc.

*Instructions continued on page 83.*

# TIME TO RELAX

**MATERIALS**

Medium Weight Yarn (4)

[3.5 ounces, 208 yards (100 grams, 190 meters) per skein]:
  13 skeins

Crochet hook, size J (6 mm) **or** size needed for gauge

━━━━▢ INTERMEDIATE

**Finished Size:** 47" x 65"
(119.5 cm x 165 cm)

**GAUGE:** In pattern, one repeat = $3^1/_2$" (9 cm);
  one row repeat (Rows 2-5) = $2^1/_2$" (6.25 cm)

**Gauge Swatch:** $7^3/_4$"w x 5"h
(19.75 cm x 12.75 cm)
Ch 25.
Work same as Afghan Body for 8 rows.
Finish off.

## STITCH GUIDE

### TREBLE CROCHET (abbreviated tr)
YO twice, insert hook in st or sp indicated, YO and pull up a loop (4 loops on hook), (YO and draw through 2 loops on hook) 3 times.
### POPCORN (uses one dc)
4 Dc in dc indicated, drop loop from hook, insert hook in first dc of 4-dc group, hook dropped loop and draw through st **(Fig. 6, page 124)**, ch 1 to close.
### PICOT
Ch 3, sc in third ch from hook.

## AFGHAN BODY

Ch 124; place marker in third ch from hook for st placement.

**Row 1** (Right side)**:** 5 Dc in sixth ch from hook **(5 skipped chs count as first dc plus 2 skipped chs)**, skip next 4 chs, 5 dc in next ch, skip next 2 chs, dc in next ch, ★ skip next 2 chs, 5 dc in next ch, skip next 4 chs, 5 dc in next ch, skip next 2 chs, dc in next ch; repeat from ★ across: 122 dc.

**Row 2:** Ch 3 **(counts as first dc, now and throughout)**, turn; ★ skip next 2 dc, 5 hdc in next dc, skip next 4 dc, 5 hdc in next dc, skip next 2 dc, dc in next dc; repeat from ★ across.

**Row 3:** Ch 3, turn; skip next hdc, 2 dc in each of next 2 hdc, skip next 2 hdc, working **around** previous row **(Fig. 7, page 124)**, tr in sp **before** next dc 2 rows **below (Fig. 8, page 124)**, skip next hdc, 2 dc in each of next 2 hdc, ★ skip next 2 hdc, working **around** previous row, tr in sp **before** next dc 2 rows **below**, work Popcorn in next dc, tr in sp **before** next dc 2 rows **below**, skip next hdc, 2 dc in each of next 2 hdc, skip next 2 hdc, working **around** previous row, tr in sp **before** next dc 2 rows **below**, skip next hdc, 2 dc in each of next 2 hdc; repeat from ★ across to last 3 sts, skip next 2 hdc, dc in last dc: 10 Popcorns, 31 tr, and 90 dc.

*Instructions continued on page 82.*

continued from TIME TO RELAX page 80

**Row 4:** Ch 3, turn; skip next 2 dc, 5 hdc in sp **before** next dc, skip next 5 sts, 5 hdc in sp **before** next dc, ★ skip next 3 sts, dc in next Popcorn, skip next 3 sts, 5 hdc in sp **before** next dc, skip next 5 sts, 5 hdc in sp **before** next dc; repeat from ★ across to last 3 dc, skip next 2 dc, dc in last dc: 122 sts.

**Row 5:** Ch 3, turn; ★ skip next 2 hdc, 5 dc in next hdc, skip next 4 hdc, 5 dc in next hdc, skip next 2 hdc, dc in next dc; repeat from ★ across.

**Rows 6-85:** Repeat Rows 2-5, 20 times; do **not** finish off.

## EDGING

**Rnd 1:** Ch 3, do **not** turn; dc in last dc on Row 85, † working in end of rows, 2 dc in each of first 4 rows, dc in next row, (2 dc in each of next 3 rows, dc in next row) across †; working in free loops of beginning ch **(Fig. 4b, page 123)**, 3 dc in first ch, 2 dc in next ch, dc in next ch and in each ch across to marked ch, 3 dc in marked ch; repeat from † to † once; working across Row 85, 3 dc in first dc, 2 dc in next dc, dc in next dc and in each dc across and in same st as first dc; join with slip st to first dc: 552 dc.

**Rnd 2:** Ch 4 **(counts as first dc, now and throughout)**, turn; dc in same st, ch 1, ★ † skip next dc, (dc in next dc, ch 1, skip next dc) across to center dc of next corner 3-dc group †, (dc, ch 1) twice in center dc; repeat from ★ 2 times **more**, then repeat from † to † once; join with slip st to first dc: 280 dc and 280 ch-1 sps.

**Rnd 3:** Slip st in next ch-1 sp, ch 2 **(counts as first hdc)**, do **not** turn; hdc in same sp, ★ † hdc in next dc, 2 hdc in next dc and in each dc across to next corner ch-1 sp †, 3 hdc in corner ch-1 sp; repeat from ★ 2 times **more**, then repeat from † to † once, hdc in same sp as first hdc; join with slip st to first hdc: 568 hdc.

**Rnd 4:** Ch 1, turn; working in Back Loops Only **(Fig. 2, page 123)**, 2 sc in same st, ★ † sc in next hdc and in each hdc across to center hdc of next corner 3-hdc group †, 3 sc in center hdc; repeat from ★ 2 times **more**, then repeat from † to † once, sc in same st as first sc; join with slip st to **both** loops of first sc: 576 sc.

**Rnd 5:** Ch 4, turn; dc in same st, ch 1, ★ † skip next sc, (dc in next sc, ch 1, skip next sc) across to center sc of next corner 3-sc group †, (dc, ch 1) twice in center sc; repeat from ★ 2 times **more**, then repeat from † to † once; join with slip st to first dc.

**Rnd 6:** Ch 7, turn; sc in third ch from hook, tr in same st as joining, (tr, work Picot, tr) in next dc and in each dc around; join with slip st to fourth ch of beginning ch-7, finish off.

*Design by Barbara Shaffer.*

**Row 3:** Ch 3 **(counts as first dc, now and throughout)**, turn; work BPdc around each of next 8 sts, ★ skip next sc, 3 dc in next FPtr, (skip next 2 sts, 3 dc in next FPtr) twice, skip next FPtr, work BPdc around each of next 8 sts; repeat from ★ across to last sc, dc in last sc.

**Rows 4-10:** Repeat Rows 2 and 3, 3 times; then repeat Row 2 once **more**.

**Row 11:** Ch 3, turn; work BPdc around each of next 8 sts, ★ (dc in next sc, ch 2, skip next 2 FPdc) 3 times, work BPdc around each of next 8 sts; repeat from ★ across to last sc, dc in last sc.

**Row 12:** Ch 1, turn; sc in first dc, work Cable twice, ★ (ch 2, skip next ch-2 sp, dc in next dc) 3 times, work Cable twice; repeat from ★ across to last dc, sc in last dc.

**Row 13:** Ch 3, turn; work BPdc around each of next 8 sts, ★ skip next dc, 3 dc in next ch, (skip next ch and next dc, 3 dc in next ch) twice, skip next ch, work BPdc around each of next 8 sts; repeat from ★ across to last sc, dc in last sc.

Repeat Rows 2-13 for pattern until Body measures approximately 68" (172.5 cm) from beginning ch, ending by working Row 10; do **not** finish off.

## EDGING

**Rnd 1:** Ch 5 **(counts as first dc plus ch 2)**, do **not** turn; working around sc at end of rows, (dc, ch 2) twice in first row, (skip next row, dc in next row, ch 2) across to last row, skip last row; working in free loops of beginning ch **(Fig. 4b, page 123)**, (dc, ch 2) 3 times in marked ch, skip next ch, dc in next ch, ch 2, (skip next 2 chs, dc in next ch, ch 2) across to last 2 chs, skip next ch, (dc, ch 2) 3 times in last ch; working around sc at end of rows, skip first row, dc in next row, ch 2, (skip next row, dc in next row, ch 2) across to last 2 rows, skip last 2 rows; working across last row, (dc, ch 2) 3 times in first sc, skip next st, dc in next st, ch 2, (skip next 2 sts, dc in next st, ch 2) across to last FPtr, skip last FPtr; join with slip st to first dc.

**Rnd 2:** Ch 5, **turn**; (dc in next dc, ch 2) around working (dc, ch 2) 3 times in each corner dc; join with slip st to first dc.

**Rnd 3:** Ch 2 **(counts as first hdc)**, do **not** turn; ★ hdc in each ch and in each dc across to next corner dc, 4 hdc in corner dc, hdc in each ch and in each dc across to next corner dc, 3 hdc in corner dc; repeat from ★ once **more**, hdc in each ch and in each dc across; join with slip st to first hdc.

**Rnd 4: Turn**; slip st in next hdc, ch 3, (2 dc, work Picot, 3 dc) in same st, skip next 2 hdc, sc in next hdc, ★ skip next 2 hdc, (3 dc, work Picot, 3 dc) in next hdc, skip next 2 hdc, sc in next hdc; repeat from ★ around to last hdc, skip last hdc; join with slip st to first dc, finish off.

*Design by Barbara Shaffer.*

# SPECIAL TIME

**MATERIALS**      **MEDIUM 4**     ◖■■■◻ INTERMEDIATE

Medium Weight Yarn
[3.5 ounces, 200 yards (100 grams, 182 meters) per skein]:
   Red - 10 skeins
   Grey - 6 skeins
Crochet hook, size J (6 mm) **or** size needed for gauge

**Finished Size:** 48" x 65"
(122 cm x 165 cm)

**GAUGE:** In pattern, 4 repeats = $3^3/_4$" (9.5 cm);
      10 rows = $3^1/_2$" (9 cm)

**Gauge Swatch:** 4"w x $4^1/_4$"h (10 cm x 10.75 cm)
Ch 14.
Work same as Afghan Body for 12 rows.
Finish off.

## STITCH GUIDE

**TREBLE CROCHET** *(abbreviated tr)*
YO twice, insert hook in sp indicated, YO and
pull up a loop (4 loops on hook), (YO and
draw through 2 loops on hook) 3 times.

**PICOT**
Ch 3, sc in third ch from hook.

## AFGHAN BODY

With Red, ch 128; place marker in second ch
from hook for st placement.

**Row 1** (Right side)**:** Sc in second ch from hook
and in each ch across changing to Grey in last sc
made *(Fig. 3a, page 123)*: 127 sc.

*Note:* Loop a short piece of yarn around any stitch
to mark Row 1 as **right** side.

**Row 2:** Ch 1, turn; sc in first sc, ★ ch 2, skip next
2 sc, sc in next sc; repeat from ★ across changing
to Red in last sc made: 43 sc and 42 ch-2 sps.

**Row 3:** Ch 1, turn; sc in first sc, 3 hdc in next
ch-2 sp and in each ch-2 sp across to last sc,
sc in last sc changing to Grey: 128 sts.

**Row 4:** Ch 1, turn; sc in first sc, ★ ch 2, skip next
2 hdc, sc in next hdc; repeat from ★ across to last
sc changing to Red in last sc made, leave last sc
unworked: 43 sc and 42 ch-2 sps.

**Rows 5-160:** Repeat Rows 3 and 4, 78 times:
43 sc and 42 ch-2 sps.

**Row 161:** Ch 1, turn; sc in first sc, 3 hdc in next
ch-2 sp and in each ch-2 sp across to last sc,
sc in last sc; do **not** finish off: 128 sts.

*Instructions continued on page 89.*

# TEA TIME

**MATERIALS**
Medium Weight Yarn **(4)**
[3.5 ounces, 205 yards (100 grams, 187 meters) per skein]:
  Blue - 13 skeins
  White - 7 skeins
Crochet hook, size J (6 mm) **or** size needed for gauge

**EASY +**

**Finished Size:** 52" x 65$\frac{1}{2}$"
(132 cm x 166.5 cm)

**GAUGE:** Each Square = 6$\frac{3}{4}$" (17.25 cm)

**Gauge Swatch:** 4$\frac{1}{2}$" (11.5 cm) square
Work same as Square through Rnd 4.

## STITCH GUIDE

**TREBLE CROCHET (abbreviated tr)**
YO twice, insert hook in st or sp
indicated, YO and pull up a loop
(4 loops on hook), (YO and draw
through 2 loops on hook) 3 times.

**LONG DOUBLE CROCHET (abbreviated Ldc)**
YO, insert hook in ch-2 sp indicated on
Rnd 1, YO and pull up a loop even with
last st made (3 loops on hook) *(Fig. A)*,
(YO and draw through 2 loops on hook)
twice.

**Fig. A**

**POPCORN** (uses one sc)
4 Dc in sc indicated, drop loop
from hook, insert hook in first dc of
4-dc group, hook dropped loop and
draw through st *(Fig. 6, page 124)*.

## SQUARE (Make 63)

With White, ch 4; join with slip st to form a ring.

**Rnd 1** (Right side): Ch 5 **(counts as first dc plus
ch 2)**, (dc in ring, ch 2) 7 times; join with slip st
to first dc, finish off: 8 dc and 8 ch-2 sps.

***Note:*** Loop a short piece of yarn around any stitch
to mark Rnd 1 as **right** side.

**Rnd 2:** With **right** side facing, join Blue with dc
in any ch-2 sp **(see Joining With Dc, page 122)**;
(2 dc, ch 1, 3 dc) in same sp, skip next ch-2 sp,
★ (3 dc, ch 1, 3 dc) in next ch-2 sp, skip next
ch-2 sp; repeat from ★ 2 times **more**; join with
slip st to first dc: 24 dc and 4 ch-1 sps.

**Rnd 3:** Ch 1, sc in same st as joining and in next
2 dc, 3 sc in next ch-1 sp, (sc in next 6 dc, 3 sc
in next ch-1 sp) 3 times, sc in last 3 dc; join with
slip st to first sc, finish off: 36 sc.

**Rnd 4:** With **right** side facing, join White with dc
in center sc of any corner 3-sc group; 3 dc in
same st, drop loop from hook, insert hook in first
dc of 4-dc group, hook dropped loop and draw
through st **(Beginning Popcorn made)**, ch 3, work
Popcorn in same st, ★ † ch 1, skip next 2 sc,
(dc, ch 2, dc) in next sc, working **around** next
2 sc **(Fig. 7, page 124)**, work 2 Ldc in ch-2 sp on
Rnd 1 **(Fig. A)**, (dc, ch 2, dc) in next sc, skip next
2 sc †, work (Popcorn, ch 3, Popcorn) in next sc;
repeat from ★ 2 times **more**, then repeat from
† to † once; join with slip st to top of Beginning
Popcorn, finish off: 32 sts and 16 sps.

*Instructions continued on page 88.*

continued from TEA TIME page 86

**Rnd 5:** With **right** side facing, join Blue with sc in any corner ch-3 sp *(see Joining With Sc, page 122)*; 2 sc in same sp, skip next Popcorn and next dc, 4 sc in next ch-2 sp, skip next dc, 2 sc in next Ldc, sc in next Ldc, 4 sc in next ch-2 sp, ★ 3 sc in next corner ch-3 sp, skip next Popcorn and next dc, 4 sc in next ch-2 sp, skip next dc, 2 sc in next Ldc, sc in next Ldc, 4 sc in next ch-2 sp; repeat from ★ 2 times **more**; join with slip st to first sc: 56 sc.

**Rnd 6:** Slip st in next sc, ch 3 **(counts as first dc)**, (2 dc, ch 1, 3 dc) in same st, ch 1, (skip next sc, dc in next sc, ch 1) 6 times, skip next sc, ★ (3 dc, ch 1, 3 dc) in next corner sc, ch 1, (skip next sc, dc in next sc, ch 1) 6 times, skip next sc; repeat from ★ 2 times **more**; join with slip st to first dc: 48 dc and 32 ch-1 sps.

**Rnd 7:** Slip st in next 2 dc and in next corner ch-1 sp, ch 1, 3 sc in same sp, sc in each dc and in each ch around working 3 sc in each corner ch-1 sp; join with slip st to first sc, finish off: 88 sc.

## ASSEMBLY

Join Squares together forming 7 vertical strips of 9 Squares each as follows:

Holding 2 Squares with **right** sides together, matching sts and working through Back Loops Only *(Fig. 2, page 123)*, join Blue with sc in center sc of any corner 3-sc group; sc in next sc and in each sc across to center sc of next corner 3-sc group, sc in center sc; finish off.

Join strips together in same manner.

## EDGING

**Rnd 1:** With **right** side facing, join White with slip st in center sc of any corner 3-sc group; ch 4 **(counts as first tr)**, (2 tr, ch 1, 3 tr) in same st, ★ † ch 1, (skip next sc, tr in next sc, ch 1) 10 times, skip next sc, [tr in next joining, ch 1, (skip next sc, tr in next sc, ch 1) 10 times, skip next sc] across to center sc of next corner 3-sc group †, (3 tr, ch 1, 3 tr) in corner sc; repeat from ★ 2 times **more**, then repeat from † to † once; join with slip st to first tr: 372 tr and 356 ch-1 sps.

**Rnd 2:** Ch 5, turn; ★ (tr in next tr, ch 1) across to next corner 6-tr group, tr in next tr, ch 2, skip next 2 tr, (3 tr, ch 1, 3 tr) in next corner ch-1 sp, ch 2, skip next 2 tr; repeat from ★ around; join with slip st to first tr, finish off: 380 tr and 364 sps.

**Rnd 3:** With **right** side facing, join Blue with sc in any corner ch-1 sp; ch 2, sc in same sp, ★ † skip next tr, (sc, ch 2, sc) in next tr, skip next tr, (sc, ch 2, sc) in next ch, skip next ch, (sc, ch 2, sc) in each tr across to ch-2 sp before next corner, skip next ch, (sc, ch 2, sc) in next ch, skip next tr, (sc, ch 2, sc) in next tr, skip next tr †, (sc, ch 2, sc) in next corner ch-1 sp; repeat from ★ 2 times **more**, then repeat from † to † once; join with slip st to first sc, finish off.

*Design by Barbara Shaffer.*

continued from SPECIAL TIME page 84

## EDGING

**Rnd 1:** Ch 3 **(counts as first dc, now and throughout)**, (2 dc, ch 1, 3 dc) in last sc on Row 161; working in end of rows, skip first row, [(dc, ch 1, dc) in next row, skip next row] across; working in free loops of beginning ch **(Fig. 4b, page 123)**, (3 dc, ch 1, 3 dc) in first ch, ★ skip next 2 chs, (dc, ch 1, dc) in next ch; repeat from ★ across to within 2 chs of marked ch, skip next 2 chs, (3 dc, ch 1, 3 dc) in marked ch; working in end of rows, skip first row, [(dc, ch 1, dc) in next row, skip next row] across; working across Row 161, skip first sc, (3 dc, ch 1, 3 dc) in next hdc, skip next 2 hdc, [(dc, ch 1, dc) in next hdc, skip next 2 hdc] across; join with slip st to first dc: 508 dc and 246 ch-1 sps.

**Rnd 2:** Turn; slip st in next dc and in next ch-1 sp, ch 4, dc in same sp, ★ (dc, ch 1, dc) in next ch-1 sp and in each ch-1 sp across to next corner ch-1 sp, ch 3, (3 dc, ch 1, 3 dc) in corner ch-1 sp, ch 3; repeat from ★ around; join with slip st to third ch of beginning ch-4.

**Rnd 3:** Turn; slip st in next 2 chs, ch 4, dc in same st, ★ † skip next ch and next dc, (dc, ch 1, dc) in next dc, (3 dc, ch 1, 3 dc) in corner ch-1 sp, skip next dc, (dc, ch 1, dc) in next dc, skip next dc and next ch, (dc, ch 1, dc) in next ch †, (dc, ch 1, dc) in next ch-1 sp and in each ch-1 sp across to next ch-3, skip next dc and next ch, (dc, ch 1, dc) in next ch; repeat from ★ 2 times **more**, then repeat from † to † once, (dc, ch 1, dc) in next ch-1 sp and in each ch-1 sp across; join with slip st to third ch of beginning ch-4.

**Rnd 4:** Turn; slip st in next dc and in next ch-1 sp, ch 1, (sc, ch 2, 2 dc) in same sp, ★ (sc, ch 2, 2 dc) in next ch-1 sp and in each ch-1 sp across to next corner ch-1 sp, dc in corner ch-1 sp, (ch 1, dc in same sp) 3 times; repeat from ★ around to last 2 ch-1 sps, (sc, ch 2, 2 dc) in last 2 ch-1 sps; join with slip st to first sc.

**Rnd 5:** Do **not** turn; (slip st, ch 1, sc) in next ch-2 sp, ★ (ch 2, sc in next ch-2 sp) across to first ch-1 sp of next corner 3 ch-1 sp group, ch 4, skip next ch-1 sp, dc in next ch-1 sp, (ch 1, dc in same sp) 5 times, ch 4, skip next ch-1 sp, sc in next ch-2 sp; repeat from ★ around to last ch-2 sp, ch 2, sc in last ch-2 sp, ch 2; join with slip st to first sc.

**Rnd 6:** Turn; (slip st, ch 4, tr) in next ch-2 sp, 2 tr in next ch-2 sp and in each sp around; join with slip st to top of beginning ch-4.

**Rnd 7:** Ch 3, turn; dc in next tr, work Picot, (dc in next 2 tr, work Picot) around; join with slip st to first dc, finish off.

*Design by Barbara Shaffer.*

# PRETTY POSIES

**MATERIALS**

**MEDIUM 4**

Medium Weight Yarn
[7 ounces, 364 yards (198 grams, 333 meters) per skein]:
  White - 5 skeins
  Green, Pink, Blue, Purple, **and** Yellow - 1 skein **each** color
Crochet hook, size I (5.5 mm) **or** size needed for gauge
³/₄" (19 mm) Button - 54
Yarn needle

■■□□ EASY

**Finished Size:** 45" x 66"
(114.5 cm x 167.5 cm)

**GAUGE:** Square Rnds 1-3 = 2¹/₂" (6.25 cm)
Each Square = 7" (17.75 cm)

## STITCH GUIDE

### TREBLE CROCHET (abbreviated tr)
YO twice, insert hook in st or sp indicated, YO and pull up a loop (4 loops on hook), (YO and draw through 2 loops on hook) 3 times.

## SQUARE (Make 54)
Make the following number of Squares using color indicated for Rnds 1, 2, 3, **and** 8: Pink - 14, Blue - 14, Purple - 13, and Yellow - 13.

With color indicated, ch 4; join with slip st to form a ring.

**Rnd 1** (Right side): Ch 1, 8 sc in ring; join with slip st to first sc.

**Rnd 2:** Ch 3, (2 tr, ch 3, slip st) in same st as joining **(Petal made)**, (slip st, ch 3, 2 tr, ch 3, slip st) in each sc around; do **not** join: 8 Petals.

**Rnd 3:** ★ Ch 4, keeping ch **behind** Petals, skip sp between next 2 Petals, slip st in sp between next 2 Petals; repeat from ★ around; do **not** join, finish off: 4 ch-4 sps.

**Rnd 4:** With **right** side facing, join Green with slip st in any ch-4 sp; ch 1, (sc, hdc, 5 dc, hdc, sc, slip st) in same sp and in each ch-4 sp around; join with slip st to first sc, finish off: 4 leaves.

*Instructions continued on page 94.*

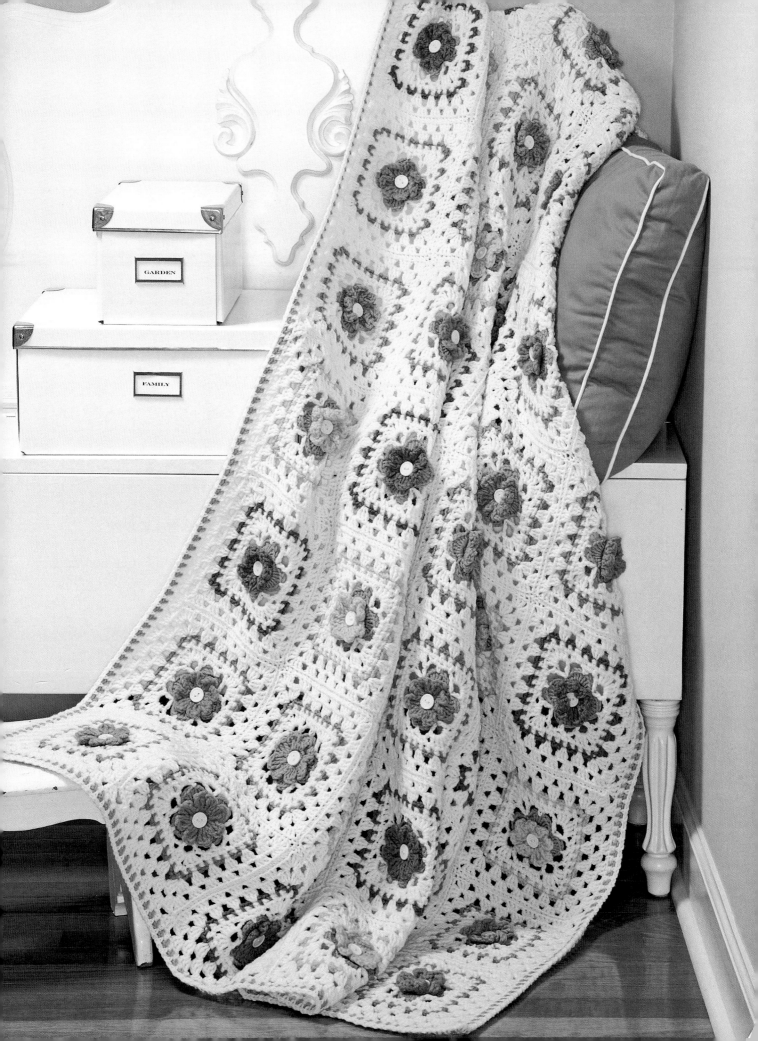

# SNOW

**MATERIALS**

Medium Weight Yarn **4** MEDIUM

[2.5 ounces, 162 yards (70 grams, 146 meters) per skein]:
22 skeins

Crochet hook, size H (5 mm) **or** size needed for gauge

◼◼◻◻ **EASY**

**Finished Size:** 48" x 64"
(122 cm x 162.5 cm)

**GAUGE:** In pattern,
16 sts and 12 rows = 4" (10 cm)

**Gauge Swatch:** 7³/₄"w x 5"h
(19.75 cm x 12.75 cm)
Ch 32.
Work same as Afghan Body for 15 rows.
Finish off.

Each row is worked across length of Afghan.

## AFGHAN BODY

Ch 256.

**Row 1:** Sc in second ch from hook, ★ ch 1, skip next ch, sc in next ch; repeat from ★ across: 128 sc and 127 ch-1 sps.

**Row 2** (Right side)**:** Ch 1, turn; sc in first sc, ch 7, sc in next sc, ★ ch 1, sc in next sc, ch 7, sc in next sc; repeat from ★ across: 64 ch-7 loops.

**Note:** Loop a short piece of yarn around any stitch to mark Row 2 as **right** side.

**Row 3:** Ch 1, turn; keeping ch-7 loops on **right** side, sc in first sc, (ch 1, sc in next sc) across: 128 sc and 127 ch-1 sps.

**Row 4:** Ch 1, turn; sc in first sc, ch 1, sc in next sc, ★ ch 7, sc in next sc, ch 1, sc in next sc; repeat from ★ across: 63 ch-7 loops.

**Row 5:** Ch 1, turn; keeping ch-7 loops on **right** side, sc in first sc, (ch 1, sc in next sc) across: 128 sc and 127 ch-1 sps.

**Row 6:** Ch 1, turn; sc in first sc, ch 7, sc in next sc, ★ ch 1, sc in next sc, ch 7, sc in next sc; repeat from ★ across: 64 ch-7 loops.

**Row 7:** Ch 1, turn; keeping ch-7 loops on **right** side, sc in first sc, (ch 1, sc in next sc) across: 128 sc and 127 ch-1 sps.

*Instructions continued on page 94.*

continued from SNOW page 92

**Row 8:** Ch 4 **(counts as first dc plus ch 1)**, turn; dc in next sc, (ch 1, dc in next sc) across.

**Row 9:** Ch 1, turn; sc in first dc, (ch 1, sc in next dc) across: 128 sc and 127 ch-1 sps.

Repeat Rows 2-9 for pattern until Afghan Body measures approximately 48" (122 cm) from beginning ch, ending by working Row 7; do **not** finish off.

## EDGING

**Rnd 1:** Ch 1, turn; slip st in next sp, (ch 1, slip st in next sp) across to last sc, (slip st, ch 3, hdc) in last sc; † working in end of rows, [skip next 2 sc rows, (slip st, ch 2, hdc) in next sc row] twice, ★ skip next dc row, (slip st, ch 2, hdc) in next sc row, [skip next 2 sc rows, (slip st, ch 2, hdc) in next sc row] twice; repeat from ★ across †; working across beginning ch, slip st in next sp, (ch 1, slip st in next sp) across to last ch, (slip st, ch 3, hdc) in free loop of last ch **(Fig. 4b, page 123)**; repeat from † to † once; join with slip st to first slip st, finish off.

*Design by Anne Halliday.*

continued from PRETTY POSIES page 90

**Rnd 5:** With **right** side facing, join White with slip st in center dc of any leaf; ch 1, sc in same st, ch 3, (dc, ch 4, dc) in slip st between next 2 leaves, ch 3, ★ sc in center dc of next leaf, ch 3, (dc, ch 4, dc) in slip st between next 2 leaves, ch 3; repeat from ★ 2 times **more**; join with slip st to first sc: 12 sts and 12 sps.

**Rnd 6:** Slip st in next ch-3 sp, ch 1, (sc, ch 1) twice in same sp, (3 dc, ch 2, 3 dc) in next ch-4 sp, ch 1, ★ (sc, ch 1) twice in each of next 2 ch-3 sps, (3 dc, ch 2, 3 dc) in next ch-4 sp, ch 1; repeat from ★ 2 times **more**, (sc, ch 1) twice in last ch-3 sp; join with slip st to first sc: 40 sts and 24 sps.

**Rnd 7:** (Slip st, ch 1, sc) in next ch-1 sp, ch 1, sc in next ch-1 sp, ch 1, skip next dc, sc in next dc, ch 1, (sc, ch 2, sc) in next corner ch-2 sp, ch 1, skip next dc, sc in next dc, ch 1, ★ (sc in next ch-1 sp, ch 1) 5 times, skip next dc, sc in next dc, ch 1, (sc, ch 2, sc) in next corner ch-2 sp, ch 1, skip next dc, sc in next dc, ch 1; repeat from ★ 2 times **more**, (sc in next ch-1 sp, ch 1) 3 times; join with slip st to first sc, finish off: 36 sc and 36 sps.

**Rnd 8:** With **right** side facing, join color indicated with slip st in any corner ch-2 sp; ch 1, (sc, ch 2, sc) in same sp, ch 1, (sc in next ch-1 sp, ch 1) 8 times, ★ (sc, ch 2, sc) in next corner ch-2 sp, ch 1, (sc in next ch-1 sp, ch 1) 8 times; repeat from ★ 2 times **more**; join with slip st to first sc, finish off: 40 sc and 40 sps.

**Rnd 9:** With **right** side facing, join White with slip st in any corner ch-2 sp; ch 3 **(counts as first dc, now and throughout)**, (2 dc, ch 2, 3 dc) in same sp, ★ † ch 1, skip next ch-1 sp, (3 dc in next ch-1 sp, ch 1, skip next ch-1 sp) 4 times †, (3 dc, ch 2, 3 dc) in next corner ch-2 sp; repeat from ★ 2 times **more**, then repeat from † to † once; join with slip st to first dc: 72 dc and 24 sps.

**Rnd 10:** Slip st in next 2 dc and in next corner ch-2 sp, ch 3, (2 dc, ch 2, 3 dc) in same sp, ch 1, (3 dc in next ch-1 sp, ch 1) 5 times, ★ (3 dc, ch 2, 3 dc) in next corner ch-2 sp, ch 1, (3 dc in next ch-1 sp, ch 1) 5 times; repeat from ★ 2 times **more**; join with slip st to first dc, finish off: 84 dc and 28 sps.

## ASSEMBLY

With White and using Placement Diagram as a guide, whipstitch Squares together forming 6 vertical strips of 9 squares each *(Fig. 9b, page 125)*, working through **inside** loops on **both** pieces, and beginning in second ch of first corner ch-2 and ending in first ch of next corner ch-2; then whipstitch strips together in same manner.

### PLACEMENT DIAGRAM

| B | A | C | D | B | A |
|---|---|---|---|---|---|
| D | C | A | B | D | C |
| C | D | B | A | C | D |
| A | B | D | C | A | B |
| B | A | C | D | B | A |
| D | C | A | B | D | C |
| C | D | B | A | C | D |
| A | B | D | C | A | B |
| B | A | C | D | B | A |

**KEY**

**A - Pink**   **B - Blue**   **C - Purple**   **D - Yellow**

## EDGING

**Rnd 1:** With **right** side of short edge facing, join White with slip st in first corner ch-2 sp; ch 3, (2 dc, ch 2, 3 dc) in same sp, ★ † ch 1, (3 dc in next ch-1 sp, ch 1) 6 times, [3 dc in end of next joining seam, ch 1, (3 dc in next ch-1 sp, ch 1) 6 times] across to next corner ch-2 sp †, (3 dc, ch 2, 3 dc) in corner ch-2 sp; repeat from ★ 2 times **more**, then repeat from † to † once; join with slip st to first dc: 642 dc and 214 sps.

**Rnd 2:** (Slip st, ch 1, sc) in next dc, ch 1, (sc, ch 2, sc) in next corner ch-2 sp, ★ † ch 1, skip next dc, sc in next dc, ch 1, [sc in next ch-1 sp, ch 1, skip next dc, sc in next dc, ch 1] across to next corner ch-2 sp †, (sc, ch 2, sc) in corner ch-2 sp; repeat from ★ 2 times **more**, then repeat from † to † once; join with slip st to first sc, finish off: 432 sc and 432 sps.

**Rnd 3:** With **right** side facing, join Green with slip st in any corner ch-2 sp; ch 1, (sc, ch 2, sc) in same sp, ★ ch 1, (sc in next ch-1 sp, ch 1) across to next corner ch-2 sp, (sc, ch 2, sc) in corner ch-2 sp; repeat from ★ 2 times **more**, ch 1, (sc in next ch-1 sp, ch 1) across; join with slip st to first sc, finish off: 436 sc and 436 sps.

**Rnd 4:** With **right** side facing, join White with slip st in any corner ch-2 sp; ch 1, (sc, ch 2, sc) in same sp, ★ ch 1, (sc in next ch-1 sp, ch 1) across to next corner ch-2 sp, (sc, ch 2, sc) in corner ch-2 sp; repeat from ★ 2 times **more**, ch 1, (sc in next ch-1 sp, ch 1) across; join with slip st to first sc, finish off.

Sew one button to center of each Square.

*Design by Maggie Weldon.*

# LACY ACCENT

## MATERIALS

Medium Weight Yarn (4) MEDIUM

[6 ounces, 315 yards (170 grams, 288 meters) per skein]:
12 skeins
Crochet hook, size K (6.5 mm) **or** size needed for gauge

**INTERMEDIATE**

**Finished Size:** 47" x 65"
(119.5 cm x 165 cm)

Afghan is worked holding two strands of yarn together.

**GAUGE:** In pattern,
one repeat (16 sts) = 6$^{1}/_{4}$" (16 cm);
5 rows = 4" (10 cm)

**Gauge Swatch:** 9"w x 4$^{1}/_{2}$"h (22.75 cm x 11.5 cm)
Ch 24.
Work same as Afghan Body for 6 rows.
Finish off.

## STITCH GUIDE

**FRONT POST TREBLE CROCHET** *(abbreviated FPtr)*
YO twice, insert hook from **front** to **back**
around post of dc indicated *(Fig. 5, page 124)*,
YO and pull up a loop (4 loops on hook), (YO
and draw through 2 loops on hook) 3 times.

**BACK POST TREBLE CROCHET** *(abbreviated BPtr)*
YO twice, insert hook from **back** to **front**
around post of dc indicated *(Fig. 5, page 124)*,
YO and pull up a loop (4 loops on hook), (YO
and draw through 2 loops on hook) 3 times.

## AFGHAN BODY

Ch 120.

**Row 1** (Right side)**:** Working in back ridges of
beginning ch *(Fig. 1, page 122)*, sc in second ch
from hook, ★ ch 1, skip next ch, sc in next ch;
repeat from ★ across: 60 sc and 59 ch-1 sps.

**Note:** Loop a short piece of yarn around any stitch
to mark Row 1 as **right** side.

**Row 2:** Ch 3 **(counts as first dc, now and
throughout)**, turn; dc in next ch-1 sp and in each
sc and each ch-1 sp across: 119 dc.

**Row 3:** Ch 3, turn; (work FPtr around next dc, dc
in next dc) 3 times, ★ ch 1, skip next 2 dc, (dc,
ch 1) twice in next dc, skip next 3 dc, (dc, ch 1)
twice in next dc, skip next 2 dc, dc in next dc,
(work FPtr around next dc, dc in next dc) 3 times;
repeat from ★ across: 84 sts and 35 ch-1 sps.

**Row 4:** Ch 3, turn; (dc in next FPtr, work BPtr
around next dc) twice, dc in next 2 sts, ★ ch 1,
skip next ch-1 sp, [(dc, ch 1) twice in next
ch-1 sp, skip next ch-1 sp] twice, dc in next
2 sts, work BPtr around next dc, dc in next FPtr,
work BPtr around next dc, dc in next 2 sts; repeat
from ★ across.

*Instructions continued on page 101.*

# LITTLE SIS

**MATERIALS**
Medium Weight Yarn (4)
[5 ounces, 260 yards (141 grams, 238 meters) per skein]:
  Blue - 9 skeins
[6 ounces, 312 yards (170 grams, 285 meters) per skein]:
  Yellow - 2 skeins
Crochet hooks, sizes I (5.5 mm) **and** J (6 mm) **or**
  sizes needed for gauge

■■■□ **INTERMEDIATE**

**Finished Size:** 51½" x 67"
(131 cm x 170 cm)

**GAUGE:** In pattern, with smaller size hook,
          one repeat from point to point
          (15 sts) = 4¼" (10.75 cm);
          Rows 3-12 = 5½" (14 cm)

**Gauge Swatch:** 8½"w x 4¼"h
                  (21.5 cm x 10.75 cm)
With Blue and smaller size hook, ch 33.
Work same as Afghan Body, page 100, for 8 rows.
Finish off.

## STITCH GUIDE

### BACK POST DOUBLE CROCHET
   *(abbreviated BPdc)*
YO, insert hook from **back** to **front** around post
of dc indicated *(Fig. 5, page 124)*, YO and pull
up a loop (3 loops on hook), (YO and draw
through 2 loops on hook) twice.

### FRONT POST DOUBLE CROCHET
   *(abbreviated FPdc)*
YO, insert hook from **front** to **back** around post
of dc indicated *(Fig. 5, page 124)*, YO and pull
up a loop (3 loops on hook), (YO and draw
through 2 loops on hook) twice.

### FRONT POST TREBLE CROCHET *(abbreviated FPtr)*
YO twice, insert hook from **front** to **back**
around post of dc indicated *(Fig. 5, page 124)*,
YO and pull up a loop (4 loops on hook), (YO
and draw through 2 loops on hook) 3 times.

### BEGINNING SC DECREASE
Pull up a loop in each of first 2 sts, YO and
draw through all 3 loops on hook (**counts as
one sc**).

### SC DECREASE
Pull up a loop in each of next 2 sts, YO and
draw through all 3 loops on hook (**counts as
one sc**).

### DC DECREASE (uses last 2 sts)
★ YO, insert hook in **next** st, YO and pull
up a loop, YO and draw through 2 loops on
hook; repeat from ★ once **more**, YO and draw
through all 3 loops on hook (**counts as one dc**).

### POPCORN (uses one ch-1 sp)
4 Dc in ch-1 sp indicated, drop loop from
hook, insert hook in first dc of 4-dc group,
hook dropped loop and draw through st *(Fig. 6,
page 124)*.

### SHELL
(3 Dc, ch 3, sc in third ch from hook, 3 dc) in
st indicated.

*Instructions continued on page 100.*

continued from LITTLE SIS page 98

## AFGHAN BODY

With Blue and smaller size hook, ch 183;
place marker in third ch from hook for Edging
placement.

**Row 1** (Wrong side): Dc in third ch from hook and
in next 6 chs, 3 dc in next ch, dc in next 6 chs,
★ skip next 2 chs, dc in next 6 chs, 3 dc in next
ch, dc in next 6 chs; repeat from ★ across to last
2 chs, dc decrease; finish off: 182 dc.

**Note:** Loop a short piece of yarn around the **back**
of any stitch on Row 1 to mark **right** side.

**Row 2:** With **right** side facing, join Yellow with
slip st in first dc; ch 2, dc in next dc, ★ † work
FPdc around next dc, work BPdc around each
of next 4 dc, work FPdc around next dc, 3 dc in
next dc, work FPdc around next dc, work BPdc
around each of next 4 dc, work FPdc around next
dc †, skip next 2 dc; repeat from ★ across to last
15 sts, then repeat from † to † once, dc decrease;
finish off.

**Row 3:** With **wrong** side facing, join Blue with
slip st in first dc; ch 2, dc in next 2 sts, ch 1,
(skip next BPdc, dc in next st, ch 1) twice, skip
next dc, 3 dc in next dc, (ch 1, skip next st, dc in
next st) 3 times, ★ skip next 2 FPdc, (dc in next
st, ch 1, skip next st) 3 times, 3 dc in next dc,
(ch 1, skip next st, dc in next st) 3 times; repeat
from ★ across to last 2 dc, dc decrease; do **not**
finish off: 110 dc and 72 chs.

**Row 4:** Ch 2, turn; dc in next dc, (work 2 FPtr
around next dc, sc in next ch) twice, skip next
dc, 3 sc in next dc, skip next dc, (sc in next ch,
work 2 FPtr around next dc) twice, ★ skip next
2 dc, (work 2 FPtr around next dc, sc in next ch)
twice, skip next dc, 3 sc in next dc, skip next dc,
(sc in next ch, work 2 FPtr around next dc) twice;
repeat from ★ across to last ch, skip last ch,
dc decrease: 182 sts.

Change to larger size hook.

**Rows 5-8:** Ch 1, turn; working in Back Loops Only
**(Fig. 2, page 123)**, beginning sc decrease, sc in
next 6 sts, 3 sc in next sc, sc in next 6 sts, ★ skip
next 2 sts, sc in next 6 sts, 3 sc in next sc, sc
in next 6 sts; repeat from ★ across to last 2 sts,
sc decrease.

Change to smaller size hook.

**Row 9:** Ch 2, turn; working in both loops, dc in
next sc, skip next sc, ★ † (dc, ch 1, dc) in next
sc, skip next 2 sc, (dc, ch 1, dc) in next sc, [skip
next sc, (dc, ch 1, dc) in next sc] twice, skip next
2 sc, (dc, ch 1, dc) in next sc †, skip next 4 sc;
repeat from ★ 10 times **more**, then repeat from
† to † once, skip next sc, dc decrease: 122 dc
and 60 ch-1 sps.

**Row 10:** Ch 2, turn; dc in next dc, (work Popcorn
in next ch-1 sp, ch 1, dc in next 2 dc) twice, 3 dc
in next ch-1 sp, (dc in next 2 dc, work Popcorn in
next ch-1 sp, ch 1) twice, ★ skip next 2 dc, (work
Popcorn in next ch-1 sp, ch 1, dc in next 2 dc)
twice, 3 dc in next ch-1 sp, (dc in next 2 dc, work
Popcorn in next ch-1 sp, ch 1) twice; repeat from
★ across to last 2 dc, dc decrease: 48 Popcorns
and 134 dc.

**Row 11:** Ch 2, turn; dc in next ch and in next
2 dc, dc in next ch and in next 3 dc, 3 dc in next
dc, dc in next 3 dc and in next ch, dc in next
2 dc, ★ skip next 2 Popcorns, dc in next 2 dc and
in next ch, dc in next 3 dc, 3 dc in next dc, dc in
next 3 dc and in next ch, dc in next 2 dc; repeat
from ★ across to last ch, dc decrease; finish off:
182 dc.

**Row 12:** With **right** side facing, join Yellow with slip st in first dc; ch 2, dc in next dc, ★ † work FPdc around next dc, work BPdc around each of next 4 dc, work FPdc around next dc, 3 dc in next dc, work FPdc around next dc, work BPdc around each of next 4 dc, work FPdc around next dc †, skip next 2 dc; repeat from ★ 10 times **more**, then repeat from † to † once, dc decrease; finish off.

**Row 13:** With **wrong** side facing, join Blue with slip st in first dc; ch 2, dc in next 7 sts, 3 dc in next dc, dc in next 6 sts, ★ skip next 2 FPdc, dc in next 6 sts, 3 dc in next dc, dc in next 6 sts; repeat from ★ across to last 2 sts, dc decrease; finish off.

**Row 14:** With **right** side facing, join Yellow with slip st in first dc; ch 2, dc in next dc, ★ † work FPdc around next dc, work BPdc around each of next 4 dc, work FPdc around next dc, 3 dc in next dc, work FPdc around next dc, work BPdc around each of next 4 dc, work FPdc around next dc †, skip next 2 dc; repeat from ★ 10 times **more**, then repeat from † to † once, dc decrease; finish off.

**Rows 15-24:** Repeat Rows 3-12.

**Rows 25-113:** Repeat Rows 3-24, 4 times; then repeat Row 13 once **more**; at end of last row, do **not** finish off.

## EDGING
Ch 1, turn; 3 sc in first dc, (skip next 3 dc, work Shell in next dc) 3 times, ★ skip next 6 dc, work Shell in next dc, (skip next 3 dc, work Shell in next dc) twice; repeat from ★ 9 times **more**, skip next 6 dc, (work Shell in next dc, skip next 3 dc) 3 times, 3 sc in last dc; sc evenly across end of rows; working in free loops of beginning ch **(Fig. 4b, page 123)**, 3 sc in marked ch, skip next 3 chs, work Shell in next ch, † skip next 6 chs, work Shell in next ch, (skip next 3 chs, work Shell in next ch) twice †; repeat from † to † 10 times **more**, skip next 6 chs, work Shell in next ch, skip next 3 chs, 3 sc in last ch; sc evenly across end of rows; join with slip st to first sc, finish off.

*Design by Barbara Shaffer.*

---

continued from LACY ACCENT page 96

**Row 5:** Ch 3, turn; (work FPtr around next dc, dc in next st) 3 times, ★ ch 1, skip next ch-1 sp, [(dc, ch 1) twice in next ch-1 sp, skip next ch-1 sp] twice, dc in next dc, (work FPtr around next dc, dc in next st) 3 times; repeat from ★ across.

**Rows 6-79:** Repeat Rows 4 and 5, 37 times.

**Row 80:** Ch 3, turn; dc in next FPtr and in each ch-1 sp and each st across: 119 dc.

**Row 81:** Ch 1, turn; sc in first dc, ★ ch 1, skip next dc, sc in next dc; repeat from ★ across; do **not** finish off.

## EDGING
Ch 1; working across end of rows, skip Row 81, slip st in top of dc on Row 80, (ch 1, slip st in top of st on next row) across, ch 2; working in sps across beginning ch, slip st in first sp, (ch 1, slip st in next sp) across, ch 2; working across end of rows, slip st in top of sc on Row 1, (ch 1, slip st in top of dc on next row) across to last row, ch 2, skip last row; working in sps across Row 81, slip st in first ch-1 sp, (ch 1, slip st in next ch-1 sp) across, ch 2; join with slip st to first slip st, finish off.

*Design by Anne Halliday.*

# TWEEDY STRIPS

## MATERIALS
Medium Weight Yarn
[7 ounces, 364 yards (198 grams, 333 meters) per skein]:
   Ecru **and** Blue - 5 skeins **each** color
   Brown **and** Dk Blue - 4 skeins **each** color
Crochet hook, size K (6.5 mm) **or** size needed for gauge
Yarn needle

**EASY +**

**Finished Size:** 52¹/₂" x 69"
(133.5 cm x 175.5 cm)

Each row is worked across length of Strips holding two strands of yarn together. When joining yarn and finishing off, leave a 9" (23 cm) end to be worked into fringe.

**GAUGE:** In pattern,
   (sc, ch 1) 4 times = 3" (7.5 cm)
   One Strip = 4"w x 69" long
   (10 cm x 175.5 cm)

**Gauge Swatch:** 4"w x 3¹/₄"h (10 cm x 8.25 cm)
Holding one strand of Ecru and one strand of Blue together, ch 10.
Work same as Strip A.

## STITCH GUIDE
### CLUSTER
Ch 3, YO, insert hook in third ch from hook, YO and pull up a loop, YO and draw through 2 loops on hook, YO, insert hook in same ch, YO and pull up a loop, YO and draw through 2 loops on hook, YO and draw through all 3 loops on hook.

## STRIP A (Make 7)
### FIRST HALF
Holding one strand of Ecru and one strand of Blue together, ch 186.

**Row 1** (Right side): Sc in second ch from hook, ★ ch 1, skip next ch, sc in next ch; repeat from ★ across; finish off: 93 sc and 92 ch-1 sps.

**Note:** Loop a short piece of yarn around any stitch to mark Row 1 as **right** side.

**Row 2:** With **wrong** side facing and holding two strands of Blue together, join yarn with sc in first sc **(see Joining With Sc, page 122)**; ★ work Cluster, skip next sc, sc in next sc; repeat from ★ across; finish off: 47 sc and 46 Clusters.

**Row 3:** With **right** side facing and holding one strand of Ecru and one strand of Blue together, join yarn with sc in first sc; ★ ch 1, working **behind** next Cluster **(Fig. 7, page 124)**, dc in sc one row **below** Cluster, ch 1, sc in next sc on Row 2; repeat from ★ across; finish off: 93 sts and 92 ch-1 sps.

**Row 4:** With **wrong** side facing and holding one strand of Ecru and one strand of Blue together, join yarn with sc in first sc; ★ ch 1, skip next ch, sc in next st; repeat from ★ across; finish off.

**Row 5:** With **right** side facing and holding one strand of Ecru and one strand of Blue together, join yarn with sc in first sc; (ch 1, sc in next sc) across; finish off.

**Row 6:** With **wrong** side facing and holding one strand of Ecru and one strand of Blue together, join yarn with sc in first sc; (ch 1, sc in next sc) across; finish off.

**Row 7:** With **right** side facing and holding two strands of Dk Blue together, join yarn with sc in first sc; (ch 1, sc in next sc) across; finish off.

*Instructions continued on page 107.*

# TWEEDY CIRCLES

## MATERIALS

Medium Weight Yarn

**4** MEDIUM

EASY +

[7 ounces, 364 yards (198 grams, 333 meters) per skein]:
  Black - 7 skeins
  Tan - 2 skeins
  Teal, Blue, Green, Plum, Brown, **and** Burgundy
    - 1 skein **each** color
[3.5 ounces, 190 yards (99 grams, 174 meters) per skein]:
  Bronze **and** Copper - 2 skeins **each** color
Crochet hook, size K (6.5 mm) **or** size needed for gauge
Yarn needle

**Finished Size:** 49" x 68"
(124.5 cm x 172.5 cm)

---

Afghan is worked holding two strands of yarn together.

**GAUGE SWATCH:** One Square = 4³/₄" (12 cm)

## SQUARE (Make 117)

Make the number of Squares indicated, working through Rnd 2 in the following colors: 23 Squares holding Teal and Tan together, 23 Squares holding Blue and Green together, 24 Squares holding Plum and Brown together, 23 Squares holding Bronze and Tan together, and 24 Squares holding Burgundy and Copper together.

Holding one strand **each** as indicated, ch 6; join with slip st to form a ring.

**Rnd 1** (Right side): Ch 3 **(counts as first dc)**, 15 dc in ring; join with slip st to first dc: 16 dc.

**Note:** Loop a short piece of yarn around any stitch to mark Rnd 1 as **right** side.

**Rnd 2:** Ch 1, (sc in next dc, ch 1) 15 times, sc in joining slip st, ch 1; join with slip st to first sc, finish off: 16 sc and 16 ch-1 sps.

**Rnd 3:** With **right** side facing, join Black with sc in any ch-1 sp **(see Joining With Sc, page 122)**; ch 1, (sc in next ch-1 sp, ch 1) around; join with slip st to first sc.

**Rnd 4:** Ch 1, sc in same st, ch 1, (dc, ch 3, dc) in next sc, ch 1, sc in next sc, ch 1, slip st in next sc, ch 1, ★ sc in next sc, ch 1, (dc, ch 3, dc) in next sc, ch 1, sc in next sc, ch 1, slip st in next sc, ch 1; repeat from ★ 2 times **more**; join with slip st to first sc, finish off: 20 sts and 20 sps.

## ASSEMBLY

With one strand of Black and working through **both** loops on **both** pieces, whipstitch Squares together in desired order **(Fig. 9a, page 125)**, forming 9 vertical strips of 13 Squares each, beginning in center ch of first corner ch-3 and ending in center ch of next corner ch-3; then whipstitch strips together in same manner.

*Instructions continued on page 106.*

continued from TWEEDY CIRCLES page 104

## EDGING

**Rnd 1:** With **right** side facing and holding two strands of Black together, join yarn with sc in any corner ch-3 sp; ch 2, sc in same sp, ch 1, ★ (sc in next sp, ch 1) across to next corner ch-3 sp, (sc, ch 2, sc) in corner ch-3 sp, ch 1; repeat from ★ 2 times **more**, (sc in next sp, ch 1) across; join with slip st to first sc: 264 sc and 264 sps.

**Rnd 2:** Ch 1, (sc, ch 2, sc) in first corner ch-2 sp, ch 1, ★ (sc in next ch-1 sp, ch 1) across to next corner ch-2 sp, (sc, ch 2, sc) in corner ch-2 sp, ch 1; repeat from ★ 2 times **more**, (sc in next ch-1 sp, ch 1) across; join with slip st to first sc, finish off: 268 sc and 268 sps.

**Rnd 3:** With **wrong** side facing and holding one strand of Teal and one strand of Tan together, join yarn with sc in any corner ch-2 sp; ch 2, sc in same sp, sc in next sc, ★ (ch 1, sc in next sc) across to next corner ch-2 sp, (sc, ch 2, sc) in corner ch-2 sp, sc in next sc; repeat from ★ 2 times **more**, (ch 1, sc in next sc) across; join with slip st to first sc, finish off: 276 sc and 268 sps.

**Rnd 4:** With **right** side facing and holding one strand of Blue and one strand of Green together, join yarn with sc in any corner ch-2 sp; ch 2, sc in same sp, ch 1, ★ skip next sc, (sc in next sc, ch 1) across to within one sc of next corner ch-2 sp, skip next sc, (sc, ch 2, sc) in next corner ch-2 sp, ch 1; repeat from ★ 2 times **more**, skip next sc, (sc in next sc, ch 1) across to last sc, skip last sc; join with slip st to first sc, finish off: 276 sc and 276 sps.

**Rnd 5:** Holding one strand of Plum and one strand of Brown together, repeat Rnd 3: 284 sc and 276 sps.

**Rnd 6:** Holding one strand of Bronze and one strand of Tan together, repeat Rnd 4: 284 sc and 284 sps.

**Rnd 7:** With **wrong** side facing and holding one strand of Burgundy and one strand of Copper together, join yarn with sc in any corner ch-2 sp; ch 2, sc in same sp, sc in next sc, ★ (ch 1, sc in next sc) across to next corner ch-2 sp, (sc, ch 2, sc) in corner ch-2 sp, sc in next sc; repeat from ★ 2 times **more**, (ch 1, sc in next sc) across; join with slip st to first sc, finish off: 292 sc and 284 sps.

**Rnd 8:** With **right** side facing and holding two strands of Black together, join yarn with sc in any corner ch-2 sp; ch 2, sc in same sp, ch 1, ★ skip next sc, (sc in next sc, ch 1) across to within one sc of next corner ch-2 sp, skip next sc, (sc, ch 2, sc) in next corner ch-2 sp, ch 1; repeat from ★ 2 times **more**, skip next sc, (sc in next sc, ch 1) across to last sc, skip last sc; join with slip st to first sc, do **not** finish off: 292 sc and 292 sps.

**Rnd 9:** (Slip st, ch 2, slip st) in first corner ch-2 sp, ch 1, ★ (slip st in next ch-1 sp, ch 1) across to next corner ch-2 sp, (slip st, ch 2, slip st) in corner ch-2 sp, ch 1; repeat from ★ 2 times **more**, (slip st in next ch-1 sp, ch 1) across; join with slip st to first slip st, finish off.

*Design by Anne Halliday.*

## SECOND HALF

**Row 1:** With **wrong** side facing, holding one strand of Ecru and one strand of Blue together, and working in free loops of beginning ch **(Fig. 4b, page 123)**, join yarn with sc in first ch; ★ ch 1, skip next ch, sc in next ch; repeat from ★ across; finish off: 93 sc and 92 ch-1 sps.

**Row 2:** With **right** side facing and holding two strands of Dk Blue together, join yarn with sc in first sc; (ch 1, sc in next sc) across; finish off.

## STRIP B (Make 6)
### FIRST HALF

Holding one strand of Ecru and one strand of Brown together, ch 186.

**Row 1 (Right side):** Sc in second ch from hook, ★ ch 1, skip next ch, sc in next ch; repeat from ★ across; finish off: 93 sc and 92 ch-1 sps.

**Note:** Mark Row 1 as **right** side.

**Row 2:** With **wrong** side facing and holding two strands of Brown together, join yarn with sc in first sc; ★ work Cluster, skip next sc, sc in next sc; repeat from ★ across; finish off: 47 sc and 46 Clusters.

**Row 3:** With **right** side facing and holding one strand of Ecru and one strand of Brown together, join yarn with sc in first sc; ★ ch 1, working **behind** next Cluster, dc in sc one row **below** Cluster, ch 1, sc in next sc on Row 2; repeat from ★ across; finish off: 93 sts and 92 ch-1 sps.

**Row 4:** With **wrong** side facing and holding one strand of Ecru and one strand of Brown together, join yarn with sc in first sc; ★ ch 1, skip next ch, sc in next st; repeat from ★ across; finish off.

**Row 5:** With **right** side facing and holding one strand of Ecru and one strand of Brown together, join yarn with sc in first sc; (ch 1, sc in next sc) across; finish off.

**Row 6:** With **wrong** side facing and holding one strand of Ecru and one strand of Brown together, join yarn with sc in first sc; (ch 1, sc in next sc) across; finish off.

**Row 7:** With **right** side facing and holding two strand of Dk Blue together, join yarn with sc in first sc; (ch 1, sc in next sc) across; finish off.

## SECOND HALF

**Row 1:** With **wrong** side facing, holding one strand of Ecru and one strand of Brown together, and working in free loops of beginning ch, join yarn with sc in first ch; ★ ch 1, skip next ch, sc in next ch; repeat from ★ across; finish off: 93 sc and 92 ch-1 sps.

**Row 2:** With **right** side facing and holding two strands of Dk Blue together, join yarn with sc in first sc; (ch 1, sc in next sc) across; finish off.

## ASSEMBLY

Alternating Strips, beginning and ending with Strip A, and placing Row 1 of Strips in the same direction, whipstitch Strips together, working through **both** loops on **both** pieces and using one strand of Dk Blue **(Fig. 9a, page 125)**.

## EDGING

With **right** side of long edge facing and holding two strands of Dk Blue together, join yarn with slip st in first sc; slip st in next sp, (ch 1, slip st in next sp) across, slip st in last sc; finish off.

Repeat Edging across second long edge.

Holding 4 strands of corresponding color yarn together, each 18" (45.5 cm) long, add additional fringe in each row across short edges of Afghan **(Figs. 10a & b, page 125)**.

*Design by Anne Halliday.*

# STARS AND STRIPES

## MATERIALS

Medium Weight Yarn **4**
[6 ounces, 278 yards (170 grams, 254 meters) per skein]:
  White - 6 skeins
  Blue - 5 skeins
  Red - 1 skein
Crochet hook, size H (5 mm) **or** size needed for gauge
Yarn needle

**■■■□** INTERMEDIATE

**Finished Size:** 54" x 71"
(137 cm x 180.5 cm)

---

**GAUGE:** One Strip = 5¼"w x 68½" long
    (13.25 cm x 174 cm)
    In pattern, one Star = 1¾" (4.5 cm)

**Gauge Swatch:** 5¼"w x 2¼"h
  (13.25 cm x 5.75 cm)
With White, make 2 Stars.
**Rnd 1:** With **right** side of first Star facing,
join Blue with sc in any ch-1 sp **(see Joining
With Sc, page 122)**; (ch 2, sc in next ch-1 sp)
4 times, ch 5; with **right** side of second
Star facing, sc in any ch-1 sp, ch 2, (sc in
next ch-1 sp, ch 2) 7 times; working across
opposite side of Stars and taking care not to
twist chs, skip first 2 chs of next ch-5, slip st
in next ch, ch 2, sc in next ch-1 sp on first
Star, ch 2, (sc in next ch-1 sp, ch 2) twice;
join with slip st to first sc, finish off.

## STITCH GUIDE

**TREBLE CROCHET (abbreviated tr)**
YO twice, insert hook in sp indicated,
YO and pull up a loop (4 loops on hook),
(YO and draw through 2 loops on hook) 3
times.
**DECREASE** (uses next 2 ch-2 sps)
★ YO 3 times, insert hook in next
ch-2 sp, YO and pull up a loop, (YO and
draw through 2 loops on hook) 3 times;
repeat from ★ once **more**, YO and draw
through all 3 loops on hook.

**EDGING DECREASE** (uses next 2 dc)
YO, insert hook in next dc, YO and pull up a loop,
YO and draw through 2 loops on hook, YO, skip
next joining, insert hook in next dc, YO and pull
up a loop, YO and draw through 2 loops on hook,
YO and draw through all 3 loops on hook.

## STAR STRIP (Make 10)

**STAR** (Make 21)
**Rnd 1** (Right side): With White, ch 5, (dc, ch 1)
7 times in fifth ch from hook **(4 skipped chs count
as first dc plus ch 1)**; join with slip st to first dc,
finish off: 8 dc and 8 ch-1 sps.

**Note:** Loop a short piece of yarn around any stitch to
mark Rnd 1 as **right** side.

## BORDER

**Rnd 1** (Right side): With **right** side of first Star facing,
join Blue with sc in any ch-1 sp **(see Joining With Sc,
page 122)**; (ch 2, sc in next ch-1 sp) 4 times, ch 5;
with **right** side of next Star facing, sc in any ch-1 sp,
[(ch 2, sc in next ch-1 sp) 3 times, ch 5; with **right**
side of next Star facing, sc in any ch-1 sp] 19 times,
ch 2, (sc in next ch-1 sp, ch 2) 7 times; working
across opposite side of Stars and taking care not
to twist chs, skip first 2 chs of next ch-5, slip st in
next ch, ch 2, sc in next ch-1 sp on next Star, [ch 2,
(sc in next ch-1 sp, ch 2) 3 times, skip first 2 chs of
next ch-5, slip st in next ch, ch 2, sc in next ch-1 sp
on next Star] 19 times, ch 2, (sc in next ch-1 sp,
ch 2) twice; join with slip st to first sc: 208 sts and
208 ch-2 sps.

*Instructions continued on page 115.*

# DOUBLE IRISH CHAIN

## MATERIALS

Medium Weight Yarn (4)
[5 ounces, 275 yards (140 grams, 251 meters) per skein]:
  Brown - 7 skeins
  Tan - 6 skeins
  Black - 3 skeins
Crochet hook, size H (5 mm) **or** size needed for gauge
Bobbins or jaw hair clips

■■■□ INTERMEDIATE

**Finished Size:** 56" x 69"
(142 cm x 175.5 cm)

**GAUGE:** In pattern, 11 hdc = 4" (10 cm);
          12 rows = 4¼" (10.75 cm)

Work hdc in space **before** next hdc *(Fig. A)* and in space **before** turning ch throughout.

**Fig. A**

**Gauge Swatch:** 4"w x 4¼"h (10 cm x 10.75 cm)
With Tan, ch 12.
**Row 1:** Hdc in second ch from hook and in each ch across: 11 hdc.
**Rows 2-12:** Ch 1, turn; hdc in first sp and in each sp across.
Finish off.

Before beginning your Afghan, please read through the Color Changing Techniques on page 114.

Wind each color onto bobbins. It is strongly recommended that you work the outlined square of the chart, page 113, as a process of familiarizing yourself with the color changes and working with bobbins. This will also aid you in determining the yardage needed for each bobbin in the design.

## AFGHAN BODY

With Brown, ch 146.

**Row 1** (Right side): Hdc in second ch from hook and in next 4 chs changing to Black in last hdc made, ★ † hdc in next 5 chs changing to Brown in last hdc made, hdc in next 5 chs changing to Tan in last hdc made, hdc in next 15 chs changing to Brown in last hdc made, hdc in next 5 chs changing to Black in last hdc made, hdc in next 5 chs changing to Brown in last hdc made †, hdc in next 5 chs changing to Tan in last hdc made, hdc in next 5 chs changing to Brown in last hdc made, hdc in next 5 chs changing to Black in last hdc made; repeat from ★ once **more**, then repeat from † to † once, hdc in last 5 chs: 145 hdc.

**Note:** Loop a short piece of yarn around any stitch to mark Row 1 as **right** side.

*Instructions continued on page 112.*

Work hdc in space **before** next hdc *(Fig. A, page 110)* and in space **before** turning ch throughout.

Continue changing colors in same manner throughout.

**Rows 2-4:** Ch 1, turn; hdc in first sp and in next 4 sps changing to Black, ★ † hdc in next 5 sps changing to Brown, hdc in next 5 sps changing to Tan, hdc in next 15 sps changing to Brown, hdc in next 5 sps changing to Black, hdc in next 5 sps changing to Brown †, hdc in next 5 sps changing to Tan, hdc in next 5 sps changing to Brown, hdc in next 5 sps changing to Black; repeat from ★ once **more**, then repeat from † to † once, hdc in last 5 sps.

**Row 5:** Ch 1, turn; hdc in first 5 sps changing to Black, ★ † hdc in next 5 sps changing to Brown, hdc in next 5 sps changing to Tan, hdc in next 15 sps changing to Brown, hdc in next 5 sps changing to Black, hdc in next 5 sps changing to Brown, hdc in next 5 sps changing to Tan †, hdc in next 5 sps changing to Brown, hdc in next 5 sps changing to Black; repeat from ★ once **more**, then repeat from † to † once.

**Rows 6-51:** Follow Chart, pages 112 & 113.

**Rows 52-185:** Follow Chart Rows 2-51 twice, then Rows 2-35 once **more**; at end of Row 185, do **not** change colors; cut Tan and Black.

On **right** side rows, work Chart from **right** to **left**; on **wrong** side rows, work Chart from **left** to **right**.

**KEY**
▲ Brown
★ Black
☐ Tan

# EDGING

**Rnd 1:** Ch 1, do **not** turn; 3 hdc in sp **before** last hdc made, working in end of rows, skip first row, hdc in next row and in each row across to last row, skip last row; working over beginning ch and in sps **before** hdc, 3 hdc in first sp and in each sp across to last sp, 3 hdc in last sp; working in end of rows, skip first row, hdc in next row and in each row across to last row, skip last row; working in sps across Row 185, 3 hdc in first sp, hdc in next sp and in each sp across; join with slip st to first hdc: 664 hdc.

**Rnd 2:** (Slip st, ch 1, hdc) in first sp, 2 hdc in next sp, ★ hdc in next sp and in each sp across to next corner 3-hdc group, 2 hdc in each of next 2 sps; repeat from ★ 2 times **more**, hdc in next sp and in each sp across, hdc in same sp as first hdc; join with slip st to first hdc.

**Rnd 3:** (Slip st, ch 1, 3 hdc) in first sp, ★ hdc in next sp and in each sp across to second hdc of first 2-hdc group, 3 hdc in next sp; repeat from ★ 2 times **more**, hdc in next sp and in each sp across; join with slip st to first hdc.

**Rnds 4 and 5:** Repeat Rnds 2 and 3.

Finish off.

*Design by Barbara Faul.*

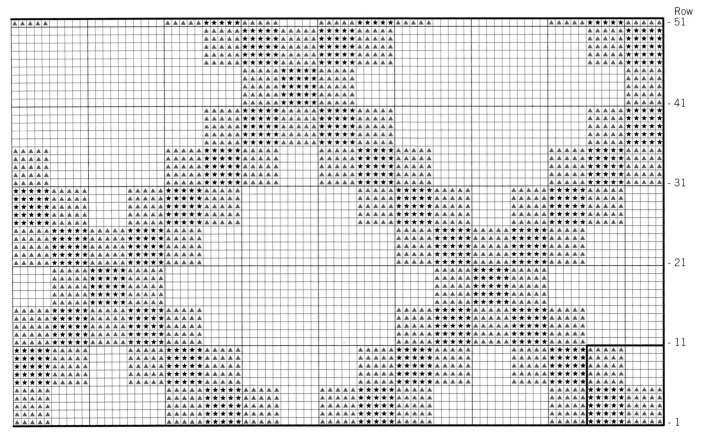

# COLOR CHANGING TECHNIQUES

## BOBBINS

Bobbins are used to hold the small amount of yarn needed to work each color change and also to help keep the different colored yarns from tangling. Start each bobbin as you would a new ball of yarn, leaving a 6" (15 cm) end to weave in later. Only unfasten enough yarn to work the area comfortably, otherwise they will tangle.

Options for Bobbins: Knitting bobbins, bobby pins, or small jaw hair clips.

## CHANGING COLORS

The basic color change is always worked the same. For the color changes to look smooth, on the row after the color change, you need to work over the strand that was created when changing colors.

Make a swatch to practice changing colors in the desired color pattern.

### BASIC COLOR CHANGE AND AT END OF ROW

YO, insert hook in st or sp indicated, YO and pull up a loop, drop yarn, with new color (*Fig. B*), YO and draw through all 3 loops on hook.

**Fig. B**

Work basic color change dropping yarn to **front** of work.

When working the **next** row, insert hook under strand of same color as space you are working into **and** in space (*Figs. C & D*).

**Fig. C**

**Fig. D**

When the yarn will be carried one stitch on the same row as the color change, insert hook in space **and** under next color (*Fig. E*).

**Fig. E**

**Rnd 2:** Ch 4 **(counts as first dc plus ch 1)**, † (dc, ch 1) 3 times in next ch-2 sp, dc in next sc, ch 1, (dc, ch 1) twice in next ch-2 sp, hdc in next ch-2 sp, ch 1, **[**(dc, ch 1, tr) in next ch-2 sp, decrease, (tr, ch 1, dc) in next ch-2 sp, ch 1, hdc in next ch-2 sp, ch 1**]** 20 times, (dc, ch 1) twice in next ch-2 sp, place marker around last dc made for st placement †, dc in next sc, ch 1, repeat from † to † once; join with slip st to first dc: 440 sts.

**Rnd 3:** Ch 1, **turn**; sc in same st as joining, ch 1, sc in next marked dc, remove marker and place around sc just made for st placement, ch 1, skip next ch, (sc in next st, ch 1, skip next st) across to next marked dc, sc in marked dc, remove marker and place around sc just made for st placement, ch 1, skip next ch, (sc in next st, ch 1, skip next st) across; join with slip st to first sc, finish off: 220 sc and 220 chs.

**Rnd 4:** With **right** side facing, join White with sc in either marked sc, remove marker; † ch 1, working **behind** next ch **(Fig. 7, page 124)**, dc in ch one rnd **below**, (sc in next sc, working **behind** next ch, dc in ch one rnd **below**) 5 times, ch 1, sc in next sc, place marker around sc just made for st placement, working **behind** next ch, dc in ch one rnd **below** †, (sc in next sc, working **behind** next ch, dc in st one rnd **below**) across to next marked sc, sc in marked sc, remove marker, repeat from † to † once, (sc in next sc, working **behind** next ch, dc in st one rnd **below**) across; join with slip st to first sc, finish off: 440 sts and 4 chs.

**Rnd 5:** With **wrong** side facing, join Red with sc in either marked sc, remove marker; † (ch 2, skip next st, sc in next st) 7 times, ch 1, skip next dc †, (sc in next sc, ch 1, skip next dc) across to next marked sc, sc in marked sc, remove marker, repeat from † to † once, (sc in next sc, ch 1, skip next dc) across; join with slip st to first sc, finish off: 222 sc and 222 sps.

**Rnd 6:** With **right** side facing and starting at either end, join White with sc in sc **before** first ch-2 sp; † place marker around sc just made for Assembly, (working **behind** next ch-2, 2 dc in st one rnd **below**, sc in next sc) 7 times, place marker around last sc made for Assembly †, (working **behind** next ch, dc in dc one rnd **below**, sc in next sc) across to next ch-2 sp, repeat from † to † once, working **behind** next ch, dc in dc one rnd **below**, (sc in next sc, working **behind** next ch, dc in dc one rnd **below**) across; join with slip st to first sc, finish off.

## ASSEMBLY

Remove markers as Strips are joined, leaving markers on outer Strips for Edging placement.

Holding two Strips with **wrong** sides together and working through **both** loops on **both** pieces, whipstitch long edge of Strips together with White **(Fig. 9a, page 125)**, beginning in first marked sc and ending in next marked sc.

Join remaining Strips in same manner.

## EDGING

With **right** side facing and working across short edge, join White with sc in marked sc; † dc in next dc, ch 2, dc in next dc, [sc in next sc, (dc in next dc, ch 2, dc in next dc, sc in next sc) 5 times, skip next dc, work edging decrease, skip next dc] 9 times, (sc in next sc, dc in next dc, ch 2, dc in next dc) 6 times, [sc in next sc, skip next dc, (dc, ch 2, dc) in next sc, skip next dc] across to next marked sc †, sc in marked sc, repeat from † to † once; join with slip st to first sc, finish off.

*Design by Anne Halliday.*

# PINWHEEL

**MATERIALS**

Medium Weight Yarn [MEDIUM 4]

[3.5 ounces, 208 yards (100 grams, 190 meters) per skein]:
  Lt Coral, Lt Green, **and** Green - 5 skeins **each** color
  Yellow and Coral - 4 skeins **each** color
Crochet hook, size H (5 mm) **or** size needed for gauge
Bobbins or jaw hair clips

◼◼◼▭ INTERMEDIATE

**Finished Size:** 59" x 67"
(150 cm x 170 cm)

**GAUGE:** In pattern, 11 hdc = 4" (10 cm);
         12 rows = $4\frac{1}{4}$" (10.75 cm)

Work hdc in space **before** next hdc *(Fig. A)* and in space **before** turning ch throughout.

**Fig. A**

**Gauge Swatch:** 4"w x $4\frac{1}{4}$"h (10 cm x 10.75 cm)
With Yellow, ch 12.
**Row 1:** Hdc in second ch from hook and in each ch across: 11 hdc.
**Rows 2-12:** Ch 1, turn; hdc in first sp and in each sp across.
Finish off.

Before beginning your Afghan, please read through the Color Changing Techniques on page 114.

Wind each color onto bobbins. It is strongly recommended that you work the outlined square of the chart, page 119, as a process of familiarizing yourself with the color changes and working with bobbins. This will also aid you in determining the yardage needed for each bobbin in the design.

## AFGHAN BODY
With Yellow, ch 153.

**Row 1** (Right side)**:** Hdc in second ch from hook and in next 18 chs changing to Green in last hdc made, hdc in next 19 chs changing to Lt Green in last hdc made, hdc in next 19 chs changing to Lt Coral in last hdc made, hdc in next 19 chs changing to Coral in last hdc made, hdc in next 19 chs changing to Yellow in last hdc made, hdc in next 19 chs changing to Green in last hdc made, hdc in next 19 chs changing to Lt Green in last hdc made, hdc in last 19 chs changing to Lt Coral in last hdc: 152 hdc.

**Note:** Loop a short piece of yarn around any stitch to mark Row 1 as **right** side.

*Instructions continued on page 120.*

On **right** side rows, work Chart from **right** to **left**; on **wrong** side rows, work Chart from **left** to **right**.

**KEY**
- ☐ Yellow
- ▲ Lt Coral
- ▼ Coral
- ◉ Lt Green
- ▣ Green

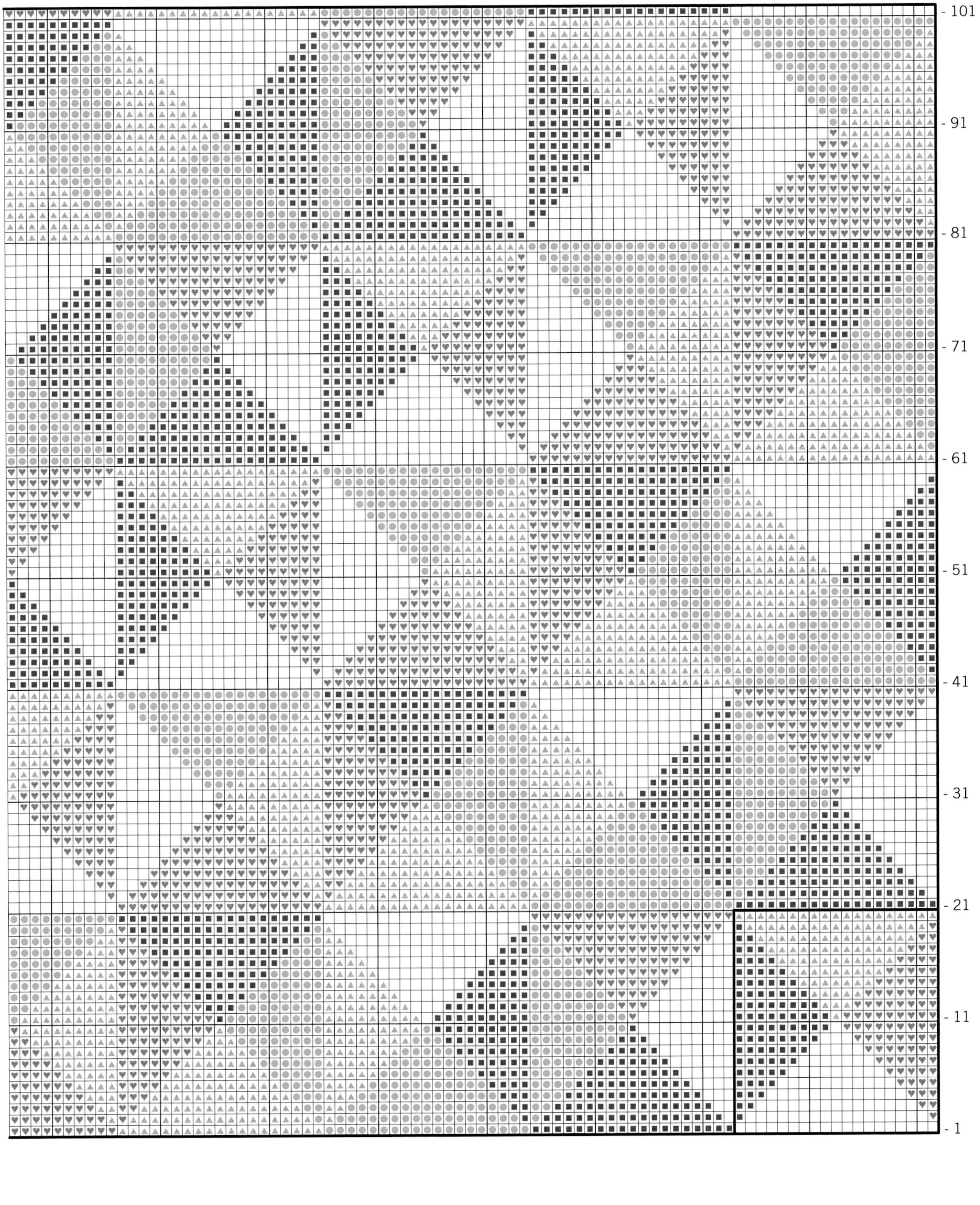

- 101
- 91
- 81
- 71
- 61
- 51
- 41
- 31
- 21
- 11
- 1

Work hdc in space **before** next hdc *(Fig. A, page 116)* and in space **before** turning ch throughout.

Continue changing colors in same manner throughout.

**Row 2:** Ch 1, turn; hdc in first sp changing to Lt Green, † hdc in next 17 sps changing to Green, hdc in next sp changing to Lt Green, hdc in next sp changing to Green, hdc in next 17 sps changing to Yellow, hdc in next sp changing to Green, hdc in next sp changing to Yellow, hdc in next 17 sps changing to Coral †, hdc in next sp changing to Yellow, hdc in next sp changing to Coral, hdc in next 17 sps changing to Lt Coral, hdc in next sp changing to Coral, hdc in next sp changing to Lt Coral, hdc in next 17 sps changing to Lt Green, hdc in next sp changing to Lt Coral, hdc in next sp changing to Lt Green, repeat from † to † once, hdc in last sp.

**Rows 3-180:** Follow Chart, pages 118 & 119, Rows 3-101 once, then Rows 2-80 once **more**; at end of Row 180, finish off Green and cut all remaining colors.

## EDGING

**Rnd 1:** With **right** side facing and working in sps across Row 180, join Yellow with hdc in first sp *(see Joining With Hdc, page 122)*; 2 hdc in same sp, hdc in next sp and in each sp across to last sp, 3 hdc in last sp; working in end of rows, skip first row, hdc in next row and in each row across to last row, skip last row; working over beginning ch and in sps **before** hdc, 3 hdc in first sp, hdc in next sp and in each sp across to last sp, 3 hdc in last sp; working in end of rows, skip first row, hdc in next row and in each row across to last row, skip last row; join with slip st to first hdc, finish off: 668 hdc.

**Rnd 2:** With **right** side facing, join Green with hdc in first sp **after** joining; 2 hdc in next sp, ★ hdc in next sp and in each sp across to next corner 3-hdc group, 2 hdc in each of next 2 sps; repeat from ★ 2 times **more**, hdc in next sp and in each sp across, hdc in same sp as first hdc; join with slip st to first hdc, finish off.

**Rnd 3:** With **right** side facing, join Lt Green with hdc in first sp **after** joining; 2 hdc in same sp, ★ hdc in next sp and in each sp across to second hdc of first 2-hdc group, 3 hdc in next sp; repeat from ★ 2 times **more**, hdc in next sp and in each sp across; join with slip st to first hdc, finish off.

**Rnd 4:** With Lt Coral, repeat Rnd 2.

**Rnd 5:** With Coral, repeat Rnd 3.

*Design by Barbara Faul.*

# GENERAL INSTRUCTIONS

## ABBREVIATIONS

| | |
|---|---|
| BLO | Back Loop(s) Only |
| BPdc | Back Post double crochet(s) |
| BPtr | Back Post treble crochet(s) |
| ch(s) | chain(s) |
| cm | centimeters |
| dc | double crochet(s) |
| dtr | double treble crochet(s) |
| FPdc | Front Post double crochet(s) |
| FPtr | Front Post treble crochet(s) |
| hdc | half double crochet(s) |
| Ldc | Long double crochet(s) |
| mm | millimeters |
| Rnd(s) | Round(s) |
| sc | single crochet(s) |
| sp(s) | space(s) |
| st(s) | stitch(es) |
| tr | treble crochet(s) |
| YO | yarn over |

★ — work instructions following ★ as many **more** times as indicated in addition to the first time.

† to † **or** ♥ to ♥ — work all instructions from first † to second † **or** from first ♥ to second ♥ **as many** times as specified.

( ) or [ ] — work enclosed instructions **as many** times as specified by the number immediately following **or** work all enclosed instructions in the stitch or space indicated **or** contains explanatory remarks.

colon (:) — the number(s) given after a colon at the end of a row or round denote(s) the number of stitches or spaces you should have on that row or round.

| CROCHET TERMINOLOGY | |
|---|---|
| **UNITED STATES** | **INTERNATIONAL** |
| slip stitch (slip st) | = single crochet (sc) |
| single crochet (sc) | = double crochet (dc) |
| half double crochet (hdc) | = half treble crochet (htr) |
| double crochet (dc) | = treble crochet(tr) |
| treble crochet (tr) | = double treble crochet (dtr) |
| double treble crochet (dtr) | = triple treble crochet (ttr) |
| triple treble crochet (tr tr) | = quadruple treble crochet (qtr) |
| skip | = miss |

| Yarn Weight Symbol & Names | LACE 0 | SUPER FINE 1 | FINE 2 | LIGHT 3 | MEDIUM 4 | BULKY 5 | SUPER BULKY 6 |
|---|---|---|---|---|---|---|---|
| Type of Yarns in Category | Fingering, 10-count crochet thread | Sock, Fingering Baby | Sport, Baby | DK, Light Worsted | Worsted, Afghan, Aran | Chunky, Craft, Rug | Bulky, Roving |
| Crochet Gauge* Ranges in Single Crochet to 4" (10 cm) | 32-42 double crochets** | 21-32 sts | 16-20 sts | 12-17 sts | 11-14 sts | 8-11 sts | 5-9 sts |
| Advised Hook Size Range | Steel*** 6,7,8 Regular hook B-1 | B-1 to E-4 | E-4 to 7 | 7 to I-9 | I-9 to K-10.5 | K-10.5 to M-13 | M-13 and larger |

*GUIDELINES ONLY: The chart above reflects the most commonly used gauges and hook sizes for specific yarn categories.

** Lace weight yarns are usually crocheted on larger-size hooks to create lacy openwork patterns. Accordingly, a gauge range is difficult to determine. Always follow the gauge stated in your pattern.

*** Steel crochet hooks are sized differently from regular hooks–the higher the number the smaller the hook, which is the reverse of regular hook sizing.

# GAUGE

Exact gauge is essential for proper size. Before beginning your project, make the sample swatch given in the individual instructions in the yarn and hook specified. After completing the swatch, measure it, counting your stitches and rows or round carefully. If your swatch is larger or smaller than specified, **make another, changing hook size to get the correct gauge**. Keep trying until you find the size hook that will give you the specified gauge.

# JOINING WITH SC

When instructed to join with sc, begin with a slip knot on hook. Insert hook in stitch or space indicated, YO and pull up a loop, YO and draw through both loops on hook.

# JOINING WITH HDC

When instructed to join with hdc, begin with a slip knot on hook. YO, holding loop on hook, insert hook in stitch or space indicated, YO and pull up a loop, YO and draw through all 3 loops on hook.

# JOINING WITH DC

When instructed to join with dc, begin with a slip knot on hook. YO, holding loop on hook, insert hook in stitch or space indicated, YO and pull up a loop (3 loops on hook), (YO and draw through 2 loops on hook) twice.

# BACK RIDGE

Work only in loops indicated by arrows *(Fig. 1)*.

**Fig. 1**

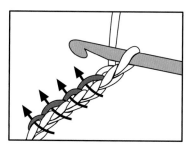

| | |
|---|---|
| ■□□□ BEGINNER | Projects for first-time crocheters using basic stitches. Minimal shaping. |
| ■■□□ EASY | Projects using yarn with basic stitches, repetitive stitch patterns, simple color changes, and simple shaping and finishing. |
| ■■■□ INTERMEDIATE | Projects using a variety of techniques, such as basic lace patterns or color patterns, mid-level shaping and finishing. |
| ■■■■ EXPERIENCED | Projects with intricate stitch patterns, techniques and dimension, such as non-repeating patterns, multi-color techniques, fine threads, small hooks, detailed shaping and refined finishing. |

| CROCHET HOOKS | | | | | | | | | | | | |
|---|---|---|---|---|---|---|---|---|---|---|---|---|
| **U.S.** | B-1 | C-2 | D-3 | E-4 | F-5 | G-6 | H-8 | I-9 | J-10 | K-10½ | N | P | Q |
| **Metric - mm** | 2.25 | 2.75 | 3.25 | 3.5 | 3.75 | 4 | 5 | 5.5 | 6 | 6.5 | 9 | 10 | 15 |

## BACK LOOP ONLY
### (abbreviated BLO)
Work only in loop(s) indicated by arrow (Fig. 2).

**Fig. 2**

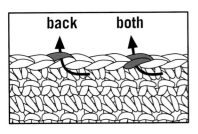

## CHANGING COLORS
Work the last stitch to within one step of completion, hook new yarn (Fig. 3a & b) and draw through both loops on hook.

**Fig. 3a**

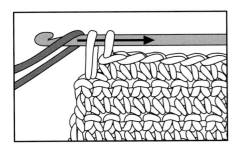

**Fig. 3b**

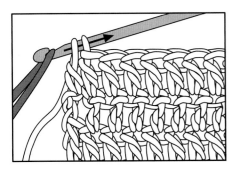

## FREE LOOPS
After working in Back or Front Loops Only on a row or round, there will be a ridge of unused loops. These are called the free loops. Later, when instructed to work in the free loops of the same row or round, work in these loops (Fig. 4a).

When instructed to work in free loops of a chain, work in loop indicated by arrow (Fig. 4b).

**Fig. 4a**

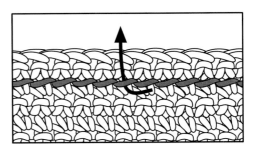

**Fig. 4b**

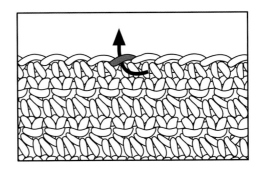

## POST STITCH

Work around the post of stitch indicated, inserting the hook in the direction of arrow *(Fig. 5)*.

**Fig. 5**

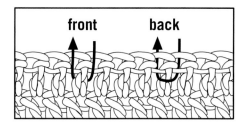

## POPCORN

Work 4 dc in stitch or space indicated, drop loop from hook, insert hook in first dc of 4-dc group, hook dropped loop and draw through stitch *(Fig. 6)*.

**Fig. 6**

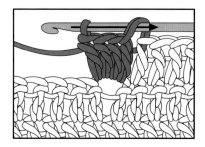

## WORKING IN FRONT OF, AROUND, OR BEHIND A STITCH

Work in stitch or space indicated, inserting hook in direction of arrow *(Fig. 7)*.

**Fig. 7**

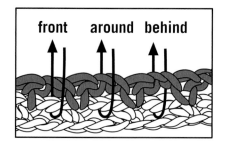

## WORKING IN A SPACE BEFORE A STITCH

When instructed to work in space **before** a stitch or in spaces **between** stitches, insert hook in space indicated by arrow *(Fig. 8)*.

**Fig. 8**

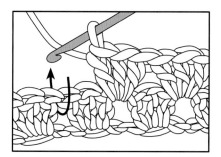

## WHIPSTITCH

Place two Squares or Strips with **wrong** sides together. Sew through both pieces once to secure the beginning of the seam, leaving an ample yarn end to weave in later. Working through **both** loops on **both** pieces or through **inside** loops on **both** pieces, insert needle from **front** to **back** through first stitch and pull yarn through *(Figs. 9a & b)*.
★ Insert the needle from **front** to **back** through next stitch on both pieces and pull yarn through; repeat from ★ across.
Repeat along the edge, being careful to match stitches and rows.

**Fig. 9a**

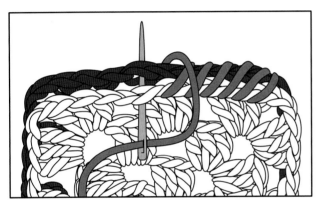

**Fig. 9b**

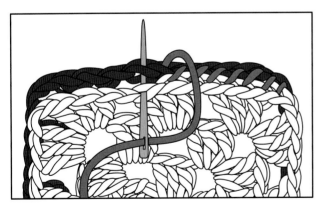

## FRINGE

Cut a piece of cardboard 8" (20.5 cm) wide and half as long as strands indicated in individual instructions. Wind the yarn **loosely** and **evenly** lengthwise around the cardboard until the card is filled, then cut across one end; repeat as needed. Hold together as many strands of yarn as specified in the individual instructions; fold in half.
With **wrong** side facing and using a crochet hook, draw the folded end up through a stitch or a row and pull the loose ends through the folded end *(Fig. 10a)*; draw the knot up **tightly** *(Fig. 10b)*.
Repeat, spacing as specified in individual instructions.
Lay flat on a hard surface and trim the ends.

**Fig. 10a**

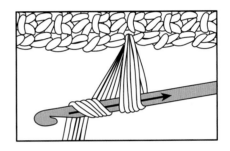

**Fig. 10b**

# Yarn Information

Each Afghan in this leaflet was made using Medium Weight or Bulky Weight yarn. Any brand of weight specified may be used. It is best to refer to the yardage/meters when determining how many balls or skeins to purchase.

Remember, to arrive at the finished size, it is the GAUGE/TENSION that is important, not the brand of yarn.

## SUNNY TWEED
**Red Heart® Super Saver®**
Dk Blue - #0380 Windsor Blue
Blue - #0382 Country Blue
White - #0316 Soft White
Yellow - #0320 Cornmeal

## ONE-OF-A-KIND
**Lion Brand® Homespun®**
Ecru - #309 Deco
Blue - #302 Colonial

## GLIMPSE OF GRANNY
**Red Heart® Soft Yarn®**
White - #7001 White
Green - #7672 Lt Yellow Green
Purple - #7582 Lt Amethyst
Teal - #7502 Lt Teal

## DENVER RIPPLE
**Lion Brand® Homespun®**
Tan - #380 Fawn
Black - #312 Edwardian
Variegated - #363 Sandstone

## CREATIVE CIRCLES
**Bernat® Berella® "4"®**
Brown - #01013 Dark Taupe
Scraps - #01210 True Aqua,
#01532 Claret, & #08886 Light
Tapestry Gold

## TILE
**Bernat® Berella® "4"®**
Taupe - #01012 True Taupe
Natural - #08940 Natural

## COMFY
**Bernat® So Soft®**
Blue - #09856 Med Blue
Lt Blue - #09854 Lt Blue

## TINY TWIRLS
**Red Heart® Super Saver®**
Ecru - #0313 Aran
Purple - #0579 Pale Plum
Pink - #0372 Rose Pink
Yellow - #0320 Cornmeal
Green - #0661 Frosty Green

## BLUE LACE
**Patons® Canadiana**
#00138 Periwinkle

## GREEK KEY
**Red Heart® Soft Yarn®**
Gold - #9114 Honey
Brown - #1882 Toast

## EXCEPTIONAL
**Patons® Décor**
Brown - #01661 Bronze
Maroon - #01657 Claret
Dk Brown - #01662 Rich
 Bronze
Cream - #01659 Pale Bronze

## NOVEMBER
**Red Heart® Super Saver®**
#0313 Aran

## CHARMING
**Red Heart® Soft Yarn®**
#382 Country Blue

## OCTOBER
**Red Heart® Super Saver®**
#0320 Cornmeal

## JAZZY JOURNEY
**Lion Brand® Jiffy®**
Lt Green - #156 Mint
Green - #181 Country Green

## SPRING SERENADE
**Red Heart® Soft Yarn®**
White - #7001 White
Teal - #7502 Lt Teal

## APRIL
**Bernat® Soft Bouclé**
Blue - #6622 Medium Blue
Variegated - #6901 Angel Fish

## OUTSTANDING
**Patons® Décor**
#01659 Pale Bronze

## HILL & VALLEY
**Lion Brand® Yarn Vanna's Choice®**
Brown - #124 Toffee
**Lion Brand® Yarn
Vanna's Choice® Baby**
Green - #169 Sweet Pea

**TRANQUILITY**
*Lion Brand® Yarn*
*Vanna's Choice® Baby*
#169 Sweet Pea

**AUTUMN**
*Patons® Canadiana*
Ecru - #00104 Aran
Brown - #00109 Brown
Green - #00057 Wicker Green
Gold - #00081 Gold

**TEMPTING TAUPE**
*Lion Brand® Yarn Vanna's Choice®*
#125 Taupe

**INCREDIBLE IN WHITE**
*TLC® Essentials™*
#2101 White

**SWEET TANGERINE**
*Red Heart® Soft Yarn®*
#4422 Tangerine

**TIME TO RELAX**
*Patons® Décor*
#1601 White

**SPECIAL TIME**
*Bernat® Satin*
Red - #04430 Bordeaux
Grey - #04046 Sterling

**TEA TIME**
*Patons® Canadiana*
Blue - #00138 Periwinkle
White - #00101 Winter White

**PRETTY POSIES**
*Red Heart® Super Saver®*
White - #0316 Soft White
Green - #0631 Light Sage
Pink - #0774 Light Raspberry
Blue - #0885 Delft Blue
Purple - #0358 Lavender
Yellow - #0235 Lemon

**SNOW**
*Lion Brand® Wool-Ease®*
#301 White/Multi

**LACY ACCENT**
*Caron® Simply Soft®*
#9703 Bone

**LITTLE SIS**
*TLC® Heathers*
Blue - #2474 Lt Denim
*TLC® Essentials™*
Yellow - #2220 Butter

**TWEEDY STRIPS**
*Red Heart® Super Saver®*
Ecru - #0313 Aran
Blue - #0382 Country Blue
Brown - #0336 Warm Brown
Dk Blue - #0380 Windsor Blue

**TWEEDY CIRCLES**
*Red Heart® Super Saver®*
Black - #0312 Black
Tan - #0334 Buff
Teal - #0388 Teal
Blue - #0380 Windsor Blue
Green - #0362 Spruce
Plum - #0533 Dk Plum
Brown - #0336 Warm Brown
Burgundy - #0376 Burgundy
*Red Heart® Classic™*
Bronze - #0286 Bronze
Copper - #0289 Copper

**STARS AND STRIPES**
*Red Heart® Plush™*
White - #9103 Cream
Blue - #9823 French Blue
Red - #9782 Wine

**DOUBLE IRISH CHAIN**
*Bernat® So Soft®*
Brown - #75029 Walnut Brown
Tan - #70522 Dk Heather
Black - #09876 Black

**PINWHEEL**
*Patons® Décor*
Yellow - #1659 Pale Bronze
Lt Coral - #1650 Pale Coralberry
Coral - #1651 Coralberry
Lt Green - #1635 Pale
  Sage Green
Green - #1636 Sage Green

# Afghan Journal

| Date | Recipient | Pattern Name | Yarn Used | Yardage | Hook Size |
|------|-----------|--------------|-----------|---------|-----------|
| | | | | | |
| | | | | | |
| | | | | | |
| | | | | | |
| | | | | | |
| | | | | | |
| | | | | | |
| | | | | | |
| | | | | | |
| | | | | | |
| | | | | | |
| | | | | | |
| | | | | | |
| | | | | | |
| | | | | | |
| | | | | | |
| | | | | | |
| | | | | | |
| | | | | | |